Interpreting in Legal Settings

Studies in Interpretation

Melanie Metzger and Earl Fleetwood, General Editors

VOLUME 1 *From Topic Boundaries to Omission: New Research on Interpretation*
Melanie Metzger, Steven Collins, Valerie Dively, and Risa Shaw, Editors

VOLUME 2 *Attitudes, Innuendo, and Regulators: Challenges of Interpretation*
Melanie Metzger and Earl Fleetwood, Editors

VOLUME 3 *Translation, Sociolinguistic, and Consumer Issues in Interpreting*
Melanie Metzger and Earl Fleetwood, Editors

VOLUME 4 *Interpreting in Legal Settings*
Debra Russell and Sandra Hale, Editors

Interpreting in Legal Settings

Debra Russell and Sandra Hale, Editors

GALLAUDET UNIVERSITY PRESS

Washington, D.C.

Studies in Interpretation

A Series Edited by Melanie Metzger and Earl Fleetwood

Gallaudet University Press
Washington, D.C. 20002
http://gupress.gallaudet.edu

Printed in the United States of America

ISBN 978-1-56368-396-1
ISSN 1545-7613

Interior design by Richard Hendel

∞ The paper used in this publication meets the minimum requirements of American National Standard for Information Sciences–Permanence of Paper for Printed Library Materials, ANSI Z39.48-1984.

Contents

Introduction, ix

Taking Liberties? Duplicity or the Dynamics of Court Interpreting, 1
Ruth Morris

Interpreting in Asylum Appeal Hearings: Roles and Norms Revisited, 26
Waltraud Kolb and Franz Pöchhacker

Court Interpreting and Face: An Analysis of a Court Interpreter's Strategies for Conveying Threats to Own Face, 51
Bente Jacobsen

Guilty or Not Guilty? An Investigation of Deaf Jurors' Access to Court Proceedings via Sign Language Interpreting, 72
Jemina Napier and David Spencer

Interpreter Preparation Conversations: Multiple Perspectives, 123
Debra Russell

Legal Interpreting and the Deaf Community in Malaysia, 148
Zubaidah Ibrahim-Bell

Contributors, 171

Index, 175

Acknowledgments

This volume explores the processes and products that result from interpretation. The collaboration among spoken and signed language interpreters continues to strengthen our understanding of the context and realities of interpreters' work, and this volume represents such a collaboration. We thank each author for their contribution and for agreeing to share their research and ideas with a broad and diverse audience. The leadership and vision demonstrated in their work will continue to inspire the field of interpreting throughout the world. We also thank all the anonymous reviewers who took time from their already full schedules to review and comment on the manuscripts. We also want to thank Melanie Metzger and Ivey Pittle Wallace for their tremendous encouragement and support in creating this volume. Finally, special thanks to Robin Demko for her role in the editing process, and to the many others close to us who offered suggestions and guidance throughout this process.

Debra Russell
Sandra Hale,
Editors

Introduction

The work of interpreters in legal settings, whether they are spoken or signed language interpreters, is filled with enormous complexity and challenges. Not only do interpreters have to manage the specialized discourse that frames legal interactions, but they must also possess strategies to ensure the participants for whom they are interpreting have access to the legal proceedings in meaningful and authentic ways via the interpretation. The interactions in which interpreters find themselves in legal settings can be technical, traumatic, ethically challenging, sometimes amusing, and frequently demanding. The pressures of providing simultaneous and consecutive interpretation amidst convoluted questions and/or responses, complex grammatical constructions, competing linguistic goals, cross-cultural ways of viewing the world, and making decisions about how best to convey the same message in the target text are just a few of the many issues facing the interpreter working in legal domains.

As with past volumes in this series on interpretation and translation, this volume endeavors to bring evidence-based practices from both signed and spoken language interpreter researchers with a particular focus on the work that occurs in legal settings. In the chapters that follow, the reader will find discussions on several topics that offer a window into the nature of interpreting in such a specialized field. We expect that the book will be of interest to students, practitioners, and educators, bringing together divergent experiences upon which to shape our evolving knowledge and practices. While the field of interpreting has grown in many countries around the world, interpreters still share the struggle to ensure their work is recognized and performed at the standard needed to provide the best possible interpretation in a mediated communication event. Our hope is that this volume will offer important insights into interpreting in legal settings, however we also believe that many of the concepts and discoveries discussed in the chapters will apply to multiple environments that interpreters encounter.

THE CONTRIBUTIONS

This volume brings together contributions from six different countries: Israel, Austria, Denmark, Australia, Malaysia, and Canada. In addition to the different geographical perspectives, they also present a diverse range of topics, theoretical underpinnings, and research methodologies, which point to a "coming of age" of the field of legal interpreting as a research discipline. The six studies reported in this volume are data-based and deal with both spoken and signed language interpreting.

Morris's chapter "Taking Liberties? Duplicity or the Dynamics of Court Interpreting" serves as a useful introduction to the volume, dealing with macro issues of court interpreting that affect most interpreters around the world. Drawing on examples from the 1987 trial of Ivan (John) Demjanjuk in Jerusalem, it highlights that often, what on the surface may appear to be breaches of the code of ethics, may be simply the result of the dynamics of the courtroom. At times interpreters may be forced to diverge from the rigid standards of interpreting to adapt to the demands placed on them. For example, there were times when the interpreters were unable to perform at their optimum level due to difficulties beyond their control, such as long and rambling questions by lawyers, overlapping speech, speed, mixed instructions, and poor acoustics. At other times, the judge would instruct them not to interpret objections or legal arguments, which clearly contravenes the requirement under the code of ethics to interpret everything. One interesting example is the judge's instruction to the interpreter to omit the flowery language and recurring formulaic expressions of deference and courtesy used by the American attorney when interpreting into Hebrew, as the discourse practices of Hebrew courtrooms do not share these conventions. On the surface, this mandate may appear to be breaching the tenet of completeness, but it can be easily argued that such omissions are indeed necessary to achieve a faithful, pragmatic rendition (cf. Hale, 2004, 2007). Interestingly, the judge was intuitively in tune with more recent theories of interpreting accuracy. Morris also notes that at times the interpreters themselves made subtle changes, some with positive or neutral effects (such as changing all references to "translate" into "interpret" when it was clearly referring to the spoken word), and some with negative, unexpected effects. One such telling example relates to the lawyer inadvertently using the term "celebration" in the utterance "celebration of the fortieth anniversary of the Treblinka uprising," which was an obvious insensitive choice. To avoid unnecessary distress to the witness, the interpreter decided to change the term to "ceremony to mark." However, the lawyer later realized he had made an inappropriate choice and apologized for using the term. This, of course, complicated matters for the interpreter, who had never interpreted the original term, leaving the witness baffled.

Unlike other studies on interpreting, the interpreters in this study were competent, professional interpreters who, for the most part, were successful in producing faithful renditions of the original utterances. Morris's use of the terms "editing" and "gatekeeping" to refer to examples from this case, bear very little resemblance to the way these terms have been used to apply to other examples of interpreting performance, where large chunks of speech are either omitted or added at will (cf. Davidson, 2000). Despite these interpreters' professional performance, the more powerful court participants showed obvious signs of contempt towards them. For example, counsel and judges who spoke the interpreters' languages would closely monitor their renditions and offer criticisms of their performance; similarly, interpreters tended to be held responsible for all misunderstandings or unclear utterances. Morris argues that judicial attitudes need to change in order for the status of the court interpreter to be elevated.

Kolb and Pöchhacker's contribution "Interpreting in Asylum Appeal Hearings: Roles and Norms Revisited" follows a similar theme to that of Morris. Although the setting is very different, the chapter also discusses interpreters' deviations from their standard role, almost 20 years after the Demjanjuk case. The data are drawn from 14 hearings, amounting to 25 hours of audio recordings of interpreted asylum hearings in Austria, recorded between October 2005 and October 2006. The study analyzes the interpreters' role and participation status, and the translational norms reflected in their renderings. With regards to the first focus, the authors found instances of interpreter alliances with the adjudicator, where the interpreters positioned themselves as members of the institution and became co-interviewers. They did this by using the inclusive "we" when interpreting questions to the applicant (when the adjudicator simply used "I"), by asking extra questions of their own accord when they felt the answers were not complete, and by constructing their own version of the statement for the record. This last interesting phenomenon resembles the abandoned practice of the police in the United Kingdom and Australia, who would construct a coherent, well-structured, chronological statement from the often loose, incoherent, and hesitant responses of the detainees (see Coulthard, 2004; Gibbons, 1990). The practice was discontinued because it made it impossible to ascertain the authorship of the statements when challenged by means of linguistic analysis. Kolb and Pöchhacker's study found similar practices from the interpreters in their sample. They also found instances of the interpreter going to the extent of specifying the punctuation marks for the benefit of the recorder. Interestingly, the study found mixed reactions from the adjudicators about the interpreters' active participation. Some asked the interpreters to not intervene with further questioning, whereas others showed little resistance.

The second focus of the study was on translational norms. The findings show a high use of the third grammatical person by interpreters but not by adjudicators, who as a general rule adhered to the first person pronoun norm. Lexical and semantic inaccuracies were also found. The authors highlight the potential detriment to the applicant such inaccuracies may have. One very useful example is the interpreter's omission of a tag question that asked the applicant to explain an obvious contradiction in his/her account. This question would have provided the applicant with the opportunity to defend his/her credibility. The omission of the tag question removed that crucial opportunity. This study makes a significant contribution to the field of legal interpreting, as it is one of the few data-based studies of interpreted asylum hearings. The authors argue for further, larger studies to be conducted in this under-researched activity type.

Bente Jacobsen's chapter presents a case study of one Danish-English interpreter working in a Danish court. Based on Brown and Levinson's (1987) theory of politeness, Jacobsen analyzes the data from the interesting perspective of face. She highlights a number of discourse practices by the interpreter that corroborate previous findings (Berk-Seligson, 2002; Hale, 2004; Rigney, 1999) and attributes the interpreter's choices to her attempts to maintain, mitigate, or enhance face among the participants. Jacobsen presents examples where the interpreter reduces the confrontational tone of inherently face-threatening questions. There are also examples of changes made to the answers to enhance the positive face of the defendant. One interesting example shows the interpreter adding the discourse markers "Well, I mean" to preface the defendant's indirect, and evasive answer. When asked "Who purchased the ticket," the defendant uses the agentless passive "I was given the ticket," which does not answer the question. Studies of the uses of discourse markers (see Schiffrin, 1988) show that "well" can be used to mark an insufficient answer. Speakers use this marker to maintain coherence and adhere to the cooperative principle (CP) (Grice, 1975), as well as to maintain face. The defendant, who was not a native speaker of English, in this example, flouted the CP by not prefacing his answer with "well." Whether this flouting was deliberate or due to Chinese being his native language, cannot be said. Nevertheless, the interpreter added the discourse marker in her interpretation, thus adding coherence and saving the defendant's positive face. Interestingly, other studies of court interpreting have shown that when interpreters interpret from English (Hale, 1999, 2004; Rigney, 1999), they tend to omit discourse markers such as "well." In this study, the interpreter does the opposite. Another interesting point raised in this article is the interpreter's manipulation of some of the utterances to save her own positive face. This finding confirms anecdotal evidence that interpreters are often fearful of being judged as incompetent if they interpret the original utterances accurately. Jacobsen suggests further research on this topic using experimental methodologies, to corroborate her qualitative analysis.

Napier and Spencer's chapter introduces the volume's section on signed language interpreting. The chapter reports the results of an innovative study with very concrete practical applications. Unlike most other studies, which have analyzed interpreting in relation to witnesses and defendants/accused, this study analyzes the effectiveness of interpreting for deaf jurors. The object of the research was to ascertain whether the courts should permit deaf citizens to participate as jurors. The results of this study indeed led the New South Wales Law Reform Commission to recommend that deaf people be permitted to serve as jurors in criminal courts. The study is also one of the few interpreting studies to use triangulation by approaching the research questions from quantitative and qualitative paradigms, using a combination of methods. These included the main experiment, followed by content and discourse analyses, and interviews.

The study is significant in demonstrating that a high level of accuracy of interpretation is achievable when interpreters are highly qualified and experienced and are provided with the adequate preparation materials and working conditions. The deaf jurors felt they were able to participate with the same level of ease as hearing jurors. The results of the comprehension test showed the performance of both groups to be very similar. These findings also shed more light into issues of juror comprehension in general, adding to the small volume of work in this area. All mock jurors (both deaf and hearing) had difficulties understanding complex legal concepts, even after the judge attempted to explain them. The authors of this chapter make a number of recommendations and useful suggestions for further research.

Another innovative research study is presented in Russell's chapter "Interpreter Preparation Conversations: Multiple Perspectives." The practice of team interpreting in settings other than conferences is rare in spoken language interpreting. It is, however, common in signed language interpreting, making this study very relevant and practical. The main justification for working in pairs is quality assurance, where interpreters are able to correct each others' errors and to relieve each other at certain intervals to avoid fatigue. This study set out to analyze the pre-trial preparation by four teams of interpreters. This included the conversations they had with each other, with the lawyers, with the deaf witness, and with the expert witness. The methodology was quasi-experimental, using a mock trial to draw the data. The performance of the teams was recorded and later analyzed. At the completion of the trial, all participants were interviewed about their respective experiences regarding the effectiveness of the pre-trial preparation conversations.

This study provides an interesting contrast to Morris's. By giving the interpreters the opportunity to speak to the other participants to explain their role and their needs, prior to the trial, the focus and some of the power was shifted to them. The interpreters in this case were setting the agenda, and the other participants were forced to take notice. It was interesting to see, however, that the interpreters' interventions were not as effective as they should have been. When addressing the lawyers, the judges, and the expert witness, the interpreters concentrated on explaining their modus operandi but tended to use their own technical jargon that was not understood by the other participants. Surprisingly, they spent little time asking the other participants about their needs, the particulars of the case, the testimony, or if they had any questions. While they welcomed the opportunity to have pre-trial discussions, the lawyers commented later that they felt the interpreters were too controlling and that they would have preferred a dialogue rather than a monologue. The lawyers and the expert witness were surprised that the interpreters did not ask much about the particulars of the case or the testimony to help them interpret. On the other hand, the deaf consumers were happy with their pre-trial conversations. These centered around sharing mutual experiences about schooling and how the sign language was learned. It seems that interpreters reacted in a friendlier, more informal manner with the deaf consumers and in a more distant and aloof way with the hearing consumers, possibly in an attempt to impress the more powerful participants.

Some unexpected results arose from the interpreters' performance during the mock trial. Although they were over conscious of their need to monitor each other to improve on accuracy, the study found that many errors were left uncorrected. In spite of this, all the consumers commented on the fact that they became distracted by the interpreters overconfirming with each other, to the extent of even suspecting their competence. In other words, although they seemed to be checking with each other excessively, to the point of annoying the consumers, they were not completely successful in identifying every error. One interesting finding was the deaf consumers' concern that interpreter errors may have been attributed to them. They appreciated it when the conversations between one interpreter and the judge were signed back to them so that they were kept informed of everything that transpired. Similarly, judges and lawyers also wanted to be kept informed of all conversations conducted in sign language. This finding is important in light of the current debates about role. It indicates that consumers of interpreting services do not want to be excluded from any part of the exchange. Other studies have shown that many practicing interpreters (who for the most part are untrained or ad hoc) often exclude the main participants by conducting independent exchanges with one or the other party (see Bolden, 2000; Angelelli, 2004). Russell makes some insightful recommendations for educators of interpreters to address the gaps found in the research.

The concluding chapter by Ibrahim-Bell "Legal Interpreting and the Deaf Community in Malaysia" makes a useful comparison between the state of spoken and signed language interpreting in Malaysia. While neither is recognized as a profession, requiring adequate training and remuneration, signed language court interpreting is in an even worse predicament than spoken language interpreting. With only seven qualified and trained signed language interpreters in the country, most deaf people receive less than adequate services. The signed language court interpreting scene reported in this final chapter stands in stark contrast with the court interpreting scene reported in chapter 1. Signed language court interpreting in Malaysia is in its infancy, and the many issues surrounding the country's complex language policies, court procedures, and general misconceptions about interpreting, make it difficult to conduct much needed research. For example, the author states that recordings are not permitted in the courtroom; hence detailed descriptive analysis of signed language interpreting performance cannot be conducted. The current study is very small, comprising only seven respondents. However, considering that there are only seven qualified signed language interpreters, it provides a useful representation of the main issues faced by these interpreters.

The findings pointed to four main concerns from the interpreters in the sample: lack of interpreting competence, the difficulty with being forced to take on multiple roles, the difficulties associated with interpreting for "illiterate" deaf people, and the poor working conditions and remuneration. Although these issues are not unique to this country, it appears that signed language interpreting in Malaysia can be safely placed at the lowest end of the continuum. The author proposes some important recommendations for the advancement of the profession in Malaysia.

REFERENCES

Angelelli, C. (2004). *Medical interpreting and cross-cultural communication.* Cambridge: Cambridge University Press.

Berk-Seligson, S. (2002). *The bilingual courtroom: Court interpreters in the judicial process.* Chicago: University of Chicago Press.

Bolden, G. (2000). Toward understanding practices of medical interpreting: interpreters' involvement in history taking. *Discourse studies* 2 (4): 387–419.

Coulthard, M. (2004). Whose voice is it? Invented and concealed dialogue in written records of verbal evidence produced by police. In J. Cotterill (Ed.), *Language in the legal process* (pp. 19–34). New York: Palgrave Macmillan.

Davidson, B. (2000). The interpreter as institutional gatekeeper: The social-linguistic role of interpreters in Spanish-English medical discourse. *Journal of Sociolinguistics 4/3*, 379–405.

Gibbons, J. (1990). Applied linguistics in court. *Applied Linguistics* 11, 229–237.

Grice, H. P. (1975). Logic and conversation. In P. Cole & J. L. Morgan (Eds.), *Syntax and semantics 3: Speech acts* (pp. 41–58). New York: Academic Press.

Hale, S. (1999) The interpreter's treatment of discourse markers in courtroom questions. *Forensic Linguistics, 6* (1), 57–82.

Hale, S. (2004). *The discourse of court interpreting: Discourse practices of the law, the witness and the interpreter.* Amsterdam: John Benjamins.

Hale, S. (2007). *Community interpreting*. Hampshire, UK: Palgrave Macmillan.

Rigney, A. (1999). Questioning in interpreted testimony. *Forensic Linguistics, 6* (1), 83–108.

Schiffrin, D. (1988). *Discourse markers*. Cambridge: Cambridge University Press.

Taking Liberties?

Duplicity or the Dynamics

of Court Interpreting

Ruth Morris

The charge of treason or duplicity is often leveled at interpreters. If honest, no practitioner can claim that an innocent error has never been made or that the speaker's intention has been never inadvertently betrayed. The legal setting introduces an additional complication—the justification (or otherwise) for providing interpreting services for a defendant or witness. Over the centuries, many lawyers and probably even more judges have doubted and at times castigated those who have claimed an inability to participate in legal proceedings without an interpreter.

Nor does judicial criticism spare the often hapless interpreter. As has been argued elsewhere (Morris, 1993, 1995), when dealing with speakers who lack native command of the language of the proceedings, the legal system theorizes that all the interpreters on whom it is *nolens volens* condemned to rely necessarily attain perfection in their performance. It bases this assumption on an ideal world in which total equivalence is automatically achieved by any individual performing interlingual interpretation in a forensic setting. It thereby discounts the ambiguities inherent in all human systems of communication because, in this idealized view, they are entirely overcome in the interpreting process. In addition, it also treats all interpreters equally, regardless of their specific qualifications, experience, and competence.

In a classic example of double standards, however, at the same time this attitude is accompanied by a tendency to demonize all those who provide interlingual interpreting services in the legal system. These individuals are therefore expected to consistently betray the court's expectations of completeness and fidelity (which the legal system defines as the Holy Grail of translating, as opposed to the suspect activity of interpreting). As

Cronin has observed in connection with the administration of empire, the "difficulty for the imperial agent is dealing with this monstrous doubleness, the potential duplicity of interpreters" (Cronin, 2002, p. 392). In the eyes of the law, as reflected in case reports, interlingual interpreters have a dualistic image: the traitor and the instrument.

THE CONTROL ISSUE

Cronin makes the point that "the central problem of translation in general and interpreting in particular, is the problem of control" (Cronin, 2002, p. 392). Ideally, the law would exclude the traitor and ignore the instrument. The following citation, by prosecution counsel Marcia Clark at the 1995 O. J. Simpson trial, is an illustrative reflection of judicial frustration with interpreters.

> The problem, though, that we were aware of, is the translator was interpreting instead of translating what she [Rosa López] was saying and changing words and cleaning up her language, not even interpreting some of the things she was saying at all. (February 27, 1995, quoted by Pym, 1999, p. 272)

In a different judicial context—a written translation of a document to be submitted to an English court—the issue has been formulated differently, but the suspicion of translators can be read even more explicitly below in Judge Stable's comments in *Dies*.[1]

> Where the words used signify not a concrete object but a conception of the mind, the process of the translator seems to be to ascertain the conception or thought which the words used in the language to be translated conjure up in his own mind, and then, having got that conception or thought clear, to re-symbolize it in words selected from the language into which it is to be translated. A possible danger, when the document to be translated is one on which legal rights depend, is ap-

1. Although the term "translator" is clearly used in the quotation from *Dies* in its technical sense to designate those who perform the written exercise of transferring meaning from one language into another, it is frequently applied, as in the Marcia Clark extract, to designate those who perform the oral exercise of interlingual interpreting also. In addition, the legal profession tends to apply the term "translation" to what it expects of court interpreters, and "interpretation" to what it wishes to reserve as its own exclusive province.

parent, inasmuch as the witness who is in theory a mere translator in practice may construe the document in the original language and then impose on the Court the construction at which he has arrived by the medium of the translation which he has selected. (*Dies v. British and International Mining and Finance Corporation Ltd.,* 1939)

The court's frustration at its powerlessness vis-à-vis translators and the product of their work is all too evident in the above quotation. Yet the ambiguity of language is such—as the law well knows—that unless a language-switcher (translator or interpreter) is allowed to present a number of alternative renderings, inevitably the outcome of any language-switching exercise will be a particular construction of the original (foreign-language) document. For example, some 150 years ago an Illinois court possessed sufficient linguistic sophistication to argue

> It cannot be the law that because an interpreter is called who is not capable of correctly translating the evidence, or from bias or partiality renders it incorrectly, that parties must be bound by it, although it may affect their most vital and important rights. (*Schnier v. People,* 1859)

The point at issue was the meaning in English of a specific German word; the outcome was the following ruling by the court.

> In all cases of such disputes, as to the meaning of a word in the foreign language, it would be proper that the court require the interpreter to give the primary meaning of all words used in connection with the word in dispute, that the jury might be enabled to determine its meaning in case of disagreement of the interpreters. (*Schnier*)

The role of linguistic experts (which the *Schnier* court equated with interpreters) was hereby validated, it being recognized that the final decision about meaning would rest, on the basis of linguistic evidence, with the jury—thereby removing ultimate power from the interpreter. Modern American case law (*Hernandez v. New York,* 1991) has not followed this approach, instead insisting that the (traditionally single) court interpreter must be the final arbiter of meaning. One Supreme Court justice even went so far as to suggest that the jury only be permitted to hear the "official translation" (*Hernandez,* Note 2 at 419). Pym makes the point that in the O. J. Simpson trial, the witness herself—Rosa López—was used as a linguistic informant, despite the misgivings of the trial judge (Pym, 1999, p. 279).

Clearly judicial identification of the existence of a problem, as in *Schnier,* does not necessarily produce a reliable remedy. Other common judicial complaints about interpreters which have been found in legal reports relate to lack of consistency in interpreted evidence (which might lead to suspicions of highly inaccurate interpretation or perjury—see *Rajnowski* at 850) or legal technicalities, such as observance of what in certain systems are vital rules of evidence.[2] Linguistic and cultural constraints, inexperience, lack of awareness, and inattention may lead to inadvertent breaking of these rules by an interpreter, as Judge Roxburgh wrote in *Trepca Mines Ltd.,*

> Theoretically an interpreter is merely a mouthpiece and not an advocate at all, but, in fact, when an interpreter translates counsel's questions into the language of the witness, what happens is that rules of evidence are broken and, unless counsel or the judge knows the language, they are powerless to prevent it. (*In re Trepca Mines Ltd.,* 1960)

An additional problem may be that the person speaking—the originator of the utterance—does not allow the interpreter to properly complete the task of completely and accurately rendering material, as Justice Roxburgh noted in his report on the case,

> When I asked the applicant what he wanted me to do he asked me, through an interpreter—I wish to emphasize that the interpreter has been very faithful in the discharge of my instructions to him; he has not attempted to conduct the case, which he has no right whatever to do, and he has done admirably because he has generally, so far as the applicant would allow him, translated the applicant's instructions; the applicant gave about 17 sentences, only one of which the interpreter was allowed to translate—to stand this case over. (*In re Trepca Mines Ltd.,* 1960)

As Judge Stable's observation in *Dies* shows very clearly, the idea that "mere translators" can have the gall—or indeed the power—to construe a document (or utterance) independently, albeit in good faith, and impose their resultant construction on a forensic body is a disturbing

2. Such rules govern the presentation of facts and proof in proceedings before a court, including in particular the rules governing the admissibility of evidence and the exclusionary rules.

concept to judicial figures. Judge Roxburgh's comments testify to a similar feeling of frustration at the situation in which judges are placed when they have to deal with an individual whose language they do not understand and an interpreter whom both common sense (Herbert's "necessary evil" [Herbert, 1952, p. 4]) and the prevailing ethos of the legal profession tend to encourage them to distrust unless convinced otherwise in a particular instance.

Court interpreters in the United States are bound, ideally, by a strict verbatim standard of performance (Gonzáles, Vásquez, and Mikkelson, 1991, p. 34), which requires them "to interpret the original source material without editing, summarizing, deleting, or adding while conserving the language level, style, tone, and intent of the speaker" (Gonzáles et al., p. 16). It is a moot point whether any interlingual interpreter can actually consistently achieve such a stringent standard; a point acknowledged by Gonzáles, who observed that "a truly verbatim interpretation is literally impossible" (p. 17), and this issue will not be addressed here. Rather, this paper will consider, drawing on examples from the 1987 trial in Jerusalem of Ivan (John) Demjanjuk, how interpreters can be placed by other participants in legal proceedings in a position in which they are required—or encouraged or allowed—to use differing degrees of power and latitude in performing their role of interlingual mediation.

THE DEMJANJUK TRIAL

Legal and Linguistic Details

The accused was a Ukrainian speaker who at the time of his trial had lived in the United States for some 35 years but was not fluent in English. The charge against the defendant was that he had been the gas-chamber operator, the notorious Ivan the Terrible, at the Treblinka death camp during World War II. There being no jury in the Israeli legal system, Demjanjuk was tried by a panel of three professional judges who had varying degrees of proficiency in English and knew no German. At the beginning of the trial, the defense team consisted of two American attorneys who knew no Hebrew or German, and were admitted to the Israeli bar for this one trial, and an Israeli lawyer who, in addition to Hebrew, spoke a fair amount of English and a little Russian. The language of the proceedings was Hebrew. One of the judges was a fluent Yiddish speaker.

The interpretation arrangements at the trial were fairly complex. Everything said in a language other than Hebrew had to be interpreted consecutively into Hebrew by the court interpreter, for the benefit of the court, the official record, the public, and the local media (the entire trial was broadcast on Israeli radio and television).[3] Everything said in a language other than English had to be interpreted simultaneously into English by a team of two interpreters sitting in a separate, soundproof booth, working either directly from the original language material or in relay from the consecutively interpreted Hebrew version for the benefit of the English-speaking defense lawyers, a number of witnesses, the public, and the international media. In addition, everything said in court by anybody other than the defendant had to be interpreted into Ukrainian by means of the whispering technique by an interpreter sitting next to the defendant.

The interpreting arrangements at the Demjanjuk trial were based on the precedent set by the war crimes trial of Adolf Eichmann, held in Jerusalem in 1961, and were determined by the judges.[4] In both cases, the language of the court and hence of the record was Hebrew. Consecutive interpretation into Hebrew ensured maximum control by the court over what was to become the record of the trial. To have provided an English version consecutively would have considerably extended the length of the proceedings. Hence, despite certain drawbacks, such as the isolation of the English interpreters in their booth one floor up (albeit with a view of the court) and the resultant lack of contact with the legal players, it was decided that the English version should be provided simultaneously. With regard to interpretation into Ukrainian, Yiddish,

3. There are two main alternatives for providing interpreted versions of material. One is to wait until the speaker has finished, and then to provide a rendering in the other language. The other is to interpret at the same time as the speaker. The first technique is called "consecutive" interpretation, because it is provided following the original material. Its disadvantage is that it effectively doubles the amount of time needed for a discussion, presentation, or examination. The advantage is that it is possible to hear—and, when necessary, electronically record—both original and interpretation separately. This can be very useful in order to check on accuracy. It is also relatively easy to spot inaccuracies so that these can be corrected—if somebody with the appropriate language skills is listening and able to comment.

4. For a comparison of the Eichmann and Demjanjuk proceedings from the interpreting point of view, see Morris (1989b) and Morris (2001).

and German, ad hoc decisions were made, based in part on logistics and in part on practical factors, including the level of experience of the interpreters concerned. In the case of an elderly Yiddish-speaking witness, the court's flexible approach led at one point to the provision of a consecutive Yiddish version by one of the trial judges, as is allowed by Israel's Code of Criminal Procedure (as opposed to the situation elsewhere, such as Belgium). This came about, not because of any deficiency in the performance of the Yiddish-Hebrew interpreter, but because the hard of hearing witness could more readily understand the booming voice and the variant of Yiddish spoken by the judge and asked the latter to interpret the questions for him.

Gatekeeping and Control of Interpreters

The original American lead defense lawyer, Mark O'Connor, found it extremely difficult to adapt to Israeli court etiquette and practice. Israeli culture is known for its tendency to bluntness, a characteristic which at times borders on the uncivil. Even in court, while certain politeness markers may be used when addressing members of the judiciary, a no-nonsense approach tends to prevail. Unaware of this, O'Connor at times annoyed the Demjanjuk bench by his flowery rhetorical habits. In an attempt to cut short the resultant lengthening effect, the somewhat testy presiding judge instructed the court interpreter to omit such material in her rendering. This direction was given despite the fact that, in accordance with Israeli legal procedure, the interpreters had been cautioned before starting work to say exactly what was said in court.[5] Clearly, however, a different standard was expected for counsel's utterances. The rules governing interpreter performance were thus shown to be relative, depending on originator, client, and situation, as well as the specific interpreter involved. The more experienced interpreters at the Demjanjuk trial learned to apply their own judgment and act as "gatekeeper" (O'Barr & O'Barr, 1976, p. 22) without explicit instructions

5. In its early years, the Israeli legal system swore both witnesses and interpreters. This was the case at the 1961 Eichmann trial. However, later a change occurred, and as a result at the later Demjanjuk trial, interpreters were "cautioned" that if they failed to produce a true rendering, they would be liable to the penalties prescribed in law.

from the bench. At times, the presiding judge deliberately edited the record, as for example when he ruled

> אין צורך לתרגם את ההתנגדות של הסניגור אוקונור כי מיד אנחנו הסברנו לו שהוא לא הבין
> במה מדובר במקרה הזה, כנראה אולי בגלל תרגום לקוי. המתרגמים יכעסו על—שאני מייחס
> כל דבר להם אבל יותר נוח.

The version of this judicial comment that appears in the English record is

> There is no need to interpret the objection of Mr. O'Connor, because we pointed out that something was unclear, perhaps because of faulty translation. The interpreters will resent that we attribute all the mistakes to them, but there it is.[6]

However, in turn, the judge's own words were modified by the interpreter. What he actually said is

> There is no need to translate defense attorney O'Connor's objection because we immediately explained to him that he did not understand the reference in this instance, apparently—perhaps because of defective translation. The translators will be angry at—that I ascribe everything to them, but it's more convenient.

The English interpreter deliberately softened the judicial comment. She toned down the statement that defense counsel had not understood something and simply indicated that something was "unclear." In addition, she used the term "resent" rather than "angry." Typically, the Hebrew is blunt, while the edges of the English rendering are somewhat rounded off. In another example of interpreter latitude, whenever it was clear that the individual was providing an oral, not a written rendering, the interpreters at the Demjanjuk trial working into Hebrew routinely replaced all references to "translator" with "מתורגמן" (metoorgeman—interpreter), while their counterparts working into English replaced "מתרגם" (metargem—translator) with "interpreter."[7]

6. March 9, 1987, afternoon session, Hebrew transcript p. 1645, English transcript p. 2093.

7. Amusingly, the Israeli tax authorities' regulations refer to "interpreters" only, not translators, probably because of the impact that the repeated use of this somewhat uncommon word in Hebrew had at the time on the Israeli public, including the author of the regulations.

In the same context of interpreter latitude, Shlesinger (1991) observes that the interpreters into Hebrew flouted the so-called "accuracy" pledge by routinely omitting recurring formulaic expressions of deference and courtesy used by the American defense lawyers, because a faithful reproduction of such formulae would have had a farcical effect in Hebrew (p. 151). Thus, by deliberately omitting material (i.e., editing or gatekeeping), a court interpreter actually served the interests of the speaker (defense counsel) by sparing him the undesirable consequences of inappropriate usage. On the face of it, the rules were broken. However, the presiding judge's own attitude and conduct variously encouraged, required, and to some extent condoned such deviations.

The gatekeeper role imposed on and assumed by the interpreter providing the consecutive Hebrew version of defense questions became particularly clear after a mid-morning recess on day 4 of the trial. In previous days, the presiding judge had instructed the court interpreter to curtail her renderings of O'Connor's questions. At this time, she adapted a practice of looking at the presiding judge to see whether he needed a Hebrew version and only provided one when instructed by him. An example of this behavior occurred on February 19, 1987 (at 11:31 A.M.) when the court clerk by mistake approached defense counsel rather than the prosecutor, while the defense lawyer was examining a prosecution witness. After the incident, the presiding judge addressed the defense counsel in English, saying "Yes—we are sorry," implying that he should continue. However, whether because he had indeed completed his question or because he wanted to collect his thoughts, the American lawyer obviously decided that this was a good time for consecutive interpretation into Hebrew. Following eye contact between bench and interpreter, the latter received an explicit instruction from the presiding judge to provide a rendering: "כן—תתרגמי." [Yes—translate]. The upshot of this ad hoc approach to the provision of interpretation is that the official written record of the trial, the Hebrew version, is incomplete. However, since Israeli court records normally neither seek nor attain verbatim standards this situation should not be viewed as serious.

Another exchange illustrates the danger of an interpreter apparently ignoring instructions from the bench or inadvertently breaking the rules. On March 11, 1987, the presiding judge objected to the wording of a question posed in English by junior counsel for the defense, and instructed the Yiddish interpreter not to interpret the question to the witness yet: "בינתיים אל תתרגם" [Don't translate yet]. However, despite this instruction the interpreter proceeded to provide the witness with a whispered Yiddish rendering of the question. This behavior was noticed by the lead defense counsel, who said, "Thanking the honorable bench and the honorable Mr. Gill, I'd just like for the record to note the fact, even though, your honor, you indicated that should not be translated the translator was translating the whole time you were speaking, your honor, to the witness."[8]

The presiding judge responded that the witness had not yet been asked to reply, and therefore it was as if the question had been neither translated nor asked. He instructed defense counsel to ask another question, observing, "אם היא תהייה מנוסחת כראוי, הרי היא תתורגם לעד" [if it is properly phrased, then it will be translated for the witness]. The upshot of this situation was that the Yiddish interpreter had to obtain instructions from the presiding judge as to whether or not to provide a version of the question for the eyewitness—a state of affairs dependent on judicial understanding of English-language material and consequent ruling on its appropriateness.[9]

This scenario was spelled out by the presiding judge some 20 minutes after the previous incident. Much of this time had involved interaction between the presiding judge and examining defense counsel as to whether questions to the witness would be allowed, based on the lawyer's incorrect inferences or inaccurate quotations from the witness's earlier testimony. The point was now made very firmly by the presiding judge.

הוא לא אמר את זה והוא אמר שהוא לא מסוגל לאומר את זה. כך שאי אפשר לבקש ממנו לאשר דבר שהוא לא אמר. שאלה אחרת. לא נשאלה שאלה לעד, אדוני צריך לתרגם אם אני לא מתערב. אם אני מתערב אז אדוני לא מתרגם לעד שום דבר. בבקשה.[10]

[He did not say that, and he said that he was not able to say that. So that it is impossible to ask him to confirm something which he did not say. Another question. No question has been asked of the witness, Sir [= you, i.e., the Yiddish-Hebrew interpreter] must translate if I do not intervene. If I intervene, then Sir does not translate anything for the witness. Please.]

8. March 11, 1987, morning session, English transcript p. 2303.

9. March 11, 1987, morning session, Hebrew transcript p. 1800, English pp. 2302–2303.

10. March 11, 1987, morning session, Hebrew transcript p. 1804.

However, as it appears in the English record, the interpreted English version of the comments from the bench, addressed first to the English-speaking defense lawyer and then to the Yiddish-Hebrew interpreter, reads

> Judge Levin: He did not say this. And he said, he wasn't in a position to do so. So he cannot really confirm something which he's not in a position to testify to. A different question. This question—You are to interpret to the witness all the time, unless I specifically tell you not to.[11]

The obtrusiveness of the interpretation itself is evident here. The judge is, first, addressing his comments to and admonishing the English-speaking examining lawyer, through the simultaneous English interpreter. Second, he is dealing with the examination process ("a different question"), possibly intending to himself ask the witness a question. Third, he is providing instructions to the Yiddish-Hebrew consecutive interpreter, through whom the eyewitness is being questioned. The consecutive interpreter, it would appear, was not interpreting to the witness what the judge was saying, presumably assuming that since the judge was admonishing defense counsel, this did not need to be rendered into Yiddish for the witness. However, when the judge presumably turned to the witness, saying "a different question," he noted that the interpreter was not doing anything, and hence gave him general instructions: interpret unless I intervene. The attendant strain on the interpreter can be imagined.

At the Demjanjuk trial, like its earlier counterpart, the 1961 trial of Adolf Eichmann, interpretation was very much a presence in its own right. At the latter, though, neither the judges nor prosecution counsel were dependent on interpretation. Here, depending on the circumstances, different trial personae had varying degrees of dependence. For example, all three judges understood English, although not all with the same degree of facility. None understood German, so that when German expert witnesses took the stand, both the bench and the defense team were at a disadvantage compared with the chief examiner on the prosecution team. In addition, the performance of the different interpreters who took part in the proceedings underwent differing degrees of interference, both in terms of language and on a personal level. Tucked away in a glass

11. March 11, 1987, morning session, English transcript p. 2308.

booth overlooking the court area, the English interpreters were literally out of sight and sometimes out of mind in the sense that their need to keep up with rapid-fire delivery was ignored by Hebrew-speaking counsel and witnesses, and only surfaced when their client reported their distress—or his own.

> The interpreter is pleading with me by the tone of her voice . . . if I could humbly and respectfully . . . the translator . . . she's never cried for mercy yet . . . the overlap and the speed. (March 19, 1987 9:23 A.M.)

The main court interpreter, working consecutively into Hebrew both for the record and for the witnesses who did not understand English, was generally treated with courtesy and consideration by all the court players, although her performance was very much guided by the dictates of the presiding judge. The interpreters into Yiddish and German for the eyewitnesses and expert witnesses respectively received mixed treatment from the bench. The interpreter who worked into German was basically ignored by all the courtroom participants. The interpreter into Yiddish, in contrast, was tightly controlled by the presiding judge, and his performance was largely monitored and corrected. There were a number of reasons for this striking difference in treatment. The Yiddish interpreter got off to a bad start by arriving late on his first day in court, having been delayed by stringent security checks, and in addition some members of the bench themselves understood Yiddish and could therefore correct his renderings. Moreover, since eyewitness testimony from the Yiddish-speaking concentration camp survivors was paramount to the trial, its interpretation was similarly of major importance. A further factor was that it was rendered into English on relay from the Hebrew version for the English-speaking members of the defense team. In contrast, less importance seemed to be attached to the German expert testimony. The same interpreters who had gained the court's trust by working into Hebrew from English also provided the Hebrew version of German. In this case, however, the English version was provided simultaneously, so that the American defense counsel understood the witness before members of the bench. In addition, prosecuting counsel had an excellent understanding of German and not infrequently, with the utmost politeness, queried (in other words identified inaccuracies in) the Hebrew consecutive version of the testimony. Hence depending on the linguistic and personal setup, interpreted renderings were variously challenged and commented on by a variety of legal actors at different stages in the proceedings.

Record-Keeping

As indicated above, gatekeeping instructions from the bench to the interpreter clearly had implications for record-keeping at the Demjanjuk trial. The "verbatim" (Walker, 1986) standards of court reporting in American courts have never been achieved in their Israeli counterparts, where until the late 1980s judges were still keeping their own longhand record and there was neither shorthand reporter nor tape-recorder. At the Demjanjuk trial, exceptionally, all material spoken out loud in open court was audio-recorded on a master tape. However, only the (separately recorded) Hebrew and English original/interpreted versions of testimony were transcribed. Hence no written version was ever produced of evidence given in Yiddish, German, and Ukrainian, nor is there any audio-recording of what was said by interpreters into those languages. More importantly, the authoritative version of the record was that in Hebrew. This was the one reviewed by the bench. Since the three members of the bench had a fairly good grasp of English, they often understood material in that language and did not necessarily need to rely on the interpretation. Indeed, sometimes the bench responded to material in English before the court interpreter managed to deliver a Hebrew-language version. Nevertheless, a Hebrew version had to be provided eventually for the public in the courtroom, the country as a whole (following the trial on television and radio), and the written record. It was obvious, however, that the court interpreter's version was at times incomplete, in part because of the behavior of the bench. Objections by defense counsel which were overruled by the bench before they had been interpreted were sometimes simply not put into Hebrew at all, and hence for the purposes of the record did not exist. The same applied to other exchanges with defense counsel where the bench did not wait for or receive a Hebrew interpretation. Due to a variety of reasons, including the bench's lack of discipline, therefore, the official Hebrew record is not a true or complete reflection of everything said in court.

For the American lawyers, accustomed to everything uttered in an American court being included verbatim in the record of proceedings unless otherwise instructed by the judge (the famous "strike that"), the editing of both the record, and their and their colleagues' own speech through the medium of interpretation was a highly disturbing practice, as reflected in the following statement by Mark O'Connor, the original lead defense counsel, "between myself and the translators—a lot is being removed as superfluous . . . preserve the record and the life of my client depends on that record. . . . We here rely on what is said here . . ." (February 25, 1987, 12:38 P.M.).

With or without "translators," O'Connor's working hypothesis was doomed from the outset in a court system not predicated on a verbatim court record. However, as the analysis in this paper shows, complex issues involving the provision of interpreted renderings certainly added to what was already a stressful situation for a defense attorney used to practicing in a markedly different legal culture.

Taking Liberties With Questions and Answers

In 1889, a Michigan supreme court justice summarized both the ideal and the local prevailing court interpreting standards.

> It is necessary, for the due course of examination, that the interpreter shall give to the witness the precise form and tenor of each question propounded, and no more or less, and that he shall in like manner translate the precise expressions of the witness. . . . It often happens that the chance interpreter who is picked up is ignorant, or otherwise not the right person, and that he takes liberties with both questions and answers. (*Rajnowski v. Detroit,* 1889)

The insightful Justice Campbell cannot be faulted in his above identification of how, ideally, a court interpreter should perform during examination of a witness; nor in his identification of how the unprofessional interpreters with whom the Michigan system was then plagued tended to perform, to the detriment of the legal process.

Even in better resourced days, however, it must be recognized that the ideal cannot always be observed. Thus sometimes in the Demjanjuk proceedings the requirement not to summarize counsel-witness exchanges was deliberately circumvented by the court interpreter because of insurmountable communication problems. The cross-examination of the first survivor of the Treblinka death camp to give evidence was marked by considerable interactional difficulties. When faithfully interpreted into Hebrew, the complex, and at times tortuous, style of the English questions posed by the defense lawyer tended to confuse the witness (who was not a native Hebrew speaker, although he had lived in Israel for many years). Despite the presiding judge's request to defense counsel to modify his style, questions remained long and rambling.

The result was that the witness frequently requested repetition of the question. The presiding judge would then repeat the question in an abridged form. On occasion the witness, treating the court interpreter as if she were personally responsible for the complex nature of the question, would ask her to split the over-long question. When the presiding judge made the point to defense counsel that the witness wanted shorter, less complicated questions, the attorney's response was that he had been "trying to speed things up," but would do as the court wished (February 23, 1987, 4:10 P.M.). It is a moot point whether he managed to do so. In any case, the witness continued to find it difficult to cope with the questions. This problem was compounded by an acoustic difficulty, since the interpreter had to speak into a fixed microphone in order to be tape-recorded, in addition to addressing her Hebrew version both to the panel of judges and to the witness, who was sitting at right angles to the bench.

By the next day (February 24, 1987), this witness's second day on the stand, his nerves were wearing thin under the strain of giving evidence which required him to relive a traumatic period in his life. Within minutes of the start of his continued cross-examination, he somewhat querulously addressed the court interpreter directly, reminding her that he had asked her to shorten the question so that perhaps then he would understand. Faced with this direct appeal, the interpreter summarized the question which had been asked, even using the third person, prefacing her version with the words "He simply wants to know . . ." She continued to use this technique as she saw fit, even though the rules require questions to be asked by the interpreter in the first person as if s/he were the examining lawyer.

The dynamics of the communicative process at the Demjanjuk trial thus led within the first six days to other participants (both professional and lay) making the main court interpreter into a gatekeeper, an editor, and a mediator. The primary rules of the interpreting situation—not to omit anything, not to edit, to preserve register, not to summarize—had been shown not to work in this particular setting and hence were discarded for the sake of communicative efficiency. No one challenged such behavior on the part of this particular interpreter. The following is a striking but not exceptional example of what therefore transpired, where italics indicate material omitted from the Hebrew rendering.

As has been the case in the past, *that we've always attempted to honor the wishes of the honorable bench,* timeliness of objections has become quite critical *in terms of when those objections were able to reach the honorable bench* as opposed to when the evidence is already a matter of record, Your Honor. We humbly submit to this Court that for us to even be able to launch ourselves to our feet in order to get the objection into the record on a timely basis, your honor—we *will respectfully* ask *exactly* what this foundation is that's being laid by *the honorable* Mr. Blatman. We have a document that has been translated, your honor, into English. We also have in the Yiddish *an alleged 1944* memoir, which *of course* the witness certainly, *if he wishes,* can identify *if* the original *is here or* a copy *that we can trace in terms of lineage and in terms of chain of custody. Now we see something entirely different,* some type of poetical rendition of the memoir, either from the memoir itself, from the witness himself, things *your honor* all of which are now developing *and I won't use the word, your honor,* into a strange situation that we're trying to sort out before *we have* the offer of proof so that *we can properly raise objection* and are able to get that objection into the record, your honor. *So we beg the court's indulgence in this regard.*[12]

אם כן העיתוי של התנגדות כבודכם כבר ראינו את זה בעבר הוא קריטי, מתי הדברים יגיעו אליכם, האם הם כבר נמצאים בפרוטוקול או שעדיין לא. עד שאנחנו עומדים על רגלינו, לפעמים זה מאוחר מדי, ואנחנו מבקשים אפוא להכניס את ההתנגדות בזמן. מבקשים גם לדעת ממר בלטמן מהו ביסוס עליו הוא מדבר. אנחנו יש לנו כאן את הדברים, את המסמך באנגלית וגם באידיש, לכאורה זכרונות. העד יכול אולי לזהות את העותק, את המקור. אבל אפשר גם כן שהדברים אינם אלא עיבוד שירי, האם זה ניתן מפי העד, האם לאו. הכל מתפתח למצב מוזר, ואנחנו מבקשים להסדיר את הדברים בטרם יוגשו הדברים כראיה, ובטרם תגיע, וכן כדי שההתנגדות לא תגיע מאוחר מידי.[13]

12. March 10, 1987, morning session, English transcript p.2172, lines 25–28 and p.2173, lines 1–20.

13. March 10, 1987, morning session, Hebrew transcript p.1705, lines 5–15.

The truncated Hebrew version may be rendered as

So the timing of the objection, your honors—we have already seen this in the past—is critical, when things reach you, are they already in the record or not yet. By the time we're on our feet, sometimes it's too late, and we therefore wish to get our objection in time. Also wish to know from Mr. Blatman what is the foundation that he's talking about. We—we have things here, the document in English and in Yiddish as well, apparently memoirs. The witness can perhaps identify the copy, the original. But it is also possible that things are simply a poetic adaptation, from the witness or not. Everything is developing into a strange situation, and we wish to sort things out before things are submitted as evidence, and before there comes—well, so that the objection will not come too late.

The interpreter in question was performing full consecutive interpretation with note-taking. Her version is substantially accurate, but abbreviated. Particularly since the bench largely understood O'Connor's point, the interpreter clearly used her judgment in order to take up one minute of the court's time instead of two. This was very obviously not a case of memory lapses or deficient technical skills on the part of this very experienced interpreter, but rather an example of gatekeeping which helped the legal proceedings advance.

Out of a combination of convenience and courtesy to foreign counsel, the presiding judge often assigned the blame for defense counsel's ostensible failures to understand to the interpreters. On day 14 of the trial, however, such courtesy was discarded as he specifically identified and rejected the American attorney's technique of using the interpreters as an excuse and pretending not to understand. Interestingly, this is an approach which witnesses are often accused of adopting, but since lawyers normally speak the language of the proceeding, it does not often apply to them. The presiding judge commented

ובכן ,אדוני או שאיננו מבין אותי או שאיננו מבין את בלטמן. הפעם אני לא מייחס את אי
ההבנה למתורגמנים, אני מייחס את אי ההבנה לאדוני שהוא ממש לא רוצה להבין את מה
שמדברים אליו .

[Well, either Sir does not understand me or he does not understand Blatman. This time I am not ascribing the misunderstanding to the interpreters, I am ascribing the misunderstanding to Sir [= you, formal usage]—that he (=you) really does not wish to understand what people are saying to him (= you).]

This was interpreted into English as

> Well, either you did not understand me or else you did not understand Mr. Blatman. This time I am not attributing the misunderstanding to the interpreters. *I am attributing it to your misunderstanding.* You simply don't want to understand what I am saying to you.[14]

The Hebrew use of formal style, avoiding the second person in addressing defense counsel, distanced the presiding judge from the American lawyer. However, since English has no stylistic equivalent, the interpreter had no choice other than to adopt a more direct approach. Perhaps in compensation, she added an omitted "Mr." before the name of the chief prosecutor. She also, whether inadvertently or deliberately, softened the judicial attribution of the misunderstanding to O'Connor personally. However, by the last sentence she had no choice other than to be as blunt as the presiding judge, but interestingly the impersonal plural becomes "I am saying" instead of the available "what is said to him." Hence the changes in the interpreter's rendering both add and remove directness.

Word Choice

The importance of specific words to the survivor eyewitnesses in the Demjanjuk proceedings should not be underestimated. On the second day of his ordeal, the first eye witness to be questioned had specifically asked the interpreter not to refer to the "upper camp" (the term used by defense counsel), but the "death camp." The interpreter (having been directly addressed by the witness) replied, justifying her behavior, that she had said what the defense lawyer said (February 24, 1987, 9:26 A.M.).

In an attempt to thwart such direct addressing by a witness, interpreters may choose to specifically distance themselves from material that they have to utter, such as a question asked through their linguistic mediation. This was the case in another World War II war crimes trial (the Lischka case) analyzed by Harris (1981). The interpreter observed in those proceedings began each of her renderings with a formula identi-

14. March 10, 1987, morning session, Hebrew transcript p.1732, English transcript p. 2210.

fying the speaker whose particular words she was about to convey, so that when a particular witness asked her why she was asking her pointless questions, she could respond that the questions were being asked by the judge and the lawyers, not by herself—the interpreter (p. 198).

On day 14 of the Demjanjuk trial, this same issue—how to designate the two camps at Treblinka—arose during the examination of another survivor. This time the second English-speaking member of the defense team, John Gill, was cross-examining a Yiddish-speaking witness. The procedure was for his English question to be rendered consecutively into Hebrew first and then put into Yiddish. Following his fellow counsel's example, he referred to the "lower camp." The witness reacted to this expression, faithfully reproduced in the Yiddish version of the question, saying "not in the lower one—in the first one, the first camp." Obligingly, Mr. Gill rephrased his question, "You were in Camp 1 for three days?" After the answer had been given and interpreted into Hebrew and English, there came the follow-up question, complete with the forbidden words, "These two and a half days or so that you were in Camp 1, or the lower camp—" Whereupon, in an attempt to forestall a negative reaction to the term by the witness, the presiding judge tersely instructed the lawyer in a mixture of Hebrew and English: "Don't say lower [in Hebrew]—"Camp 1" [in English]" (March 10, 1987, 4:51 P.M.). Interestingly, no trace of this linguistically "hybrid" correction appears in the Hebrew transcript, only in the English, where it appears, inaccurately, as "Camp 1. Please say Camp 1."

The question is whether the interpreter—knowing that the witness objected to the phrase, that the bench was trying to prevent the lawyer from using it, and that if it were faithfully rendered in questioning the witness there would be another outburst—can truly be considered to be flouting the "rules" by replacing the reference to the "lower camp" with "Camp 1" (particularly when the presiding judge has pleaded with the lawyer to refrain from using those words), or simply omitting it. Linguistic research indicates that the way in which something is expressed can be just as important as the substance or content of what is said (Loftus, 1974). In this case, did the lawyer really intend to distress the witness by using a term to which the latter objected? Was the interpreter really thwarting the lawyer's stratagem? Would a jury have been adversely influenced by the interpreter's behavior? Was the interpreter showing solidarity with the witness or protecting the lawyer? Had the interpreter, as a member of a professional court interpreting body, been bound by a code of ethics (none of which existed at the time in Israel, nor do they exist there at the time of writing), what would her position have been in so "editing" material?

In taking liberties with forms of questioning used by counsel for the defense, the Hebrew court interpreter was clearly seeking to enhance the effectiveness of the communicative process. At one point, however, her desire to avoid upsetting the witness was responsible for a terminological choice which, while initially achieving its goal, actually generated subsequent complications when the original speaker belatedly realized his error. The original term designated events organized by survivors 40 years after the uprising of the Treblinka death camp inmates—an uprising in which most participants perished. The defense lawyer referred to the "celebration of the fortieth anniversary of the Treblinka uprising." The court interpreter realized the inappropriate nature of the lawyer's term, which would probably lead to an outburst on the part of the witness, who was already greatly overwrought. As a result, she applied the latitude already conferred on her by bench and witness alike, and replaced the term "celebration" with a Hebrew paraphrase meaning "ceremony to mark" (טקס לציון). All would have been well had the defense lawyer not belatedly realized the inappropriateness of his term "celebration," and specifically corrected it by stating that he had not meant a celebration. On the horns of this particular dilemma, the hapless interpreter then had no choice other than to repeat the lawyer's self-correction, this time being forced to use the term "celebration" (חגיגה) in Hebrew. Not having had conveyed to him the original reference to a "celebration," due to the interpreter's (arguably misplaced but understandable) delicacy, the witness was baffled. Understandably missing the point, the defense lawyer commented that he had to be very careful as to the words used by him, "because they cannot always be translated into Hebrew" (February 24, 1987, 4:28 P.M.). It is, of course, to avoid such complications that rules about interpreting tend to state baldly that there should be no deletions, additions, or editing. Yet the Catch-22 nature of the interpreter's situation can be readily understood from these few examples.

Berk-Seligson (1999, p. 49) has concluded that "interpreters often try to make the witness for whom they are interpreting feel more comfortable, or less intimidated, by the situation in which the latter finds him/herself." However, she suggests that an "unconscious motivation" is at work. In the above instance, both the interpreter's motivation and her ensuing behavior were clearly conscious and intentional.

Speed and Acoustics

Speed and acoustics were further variables that were observed to affect comprehension of interpreted material as well as reactions to examination through an interpreter at the Demjanjuk trial. Certain participants were notorious for failing to curb their naturally rapid delivery. Early in the trial, defense counsel even went so far as to "apologize to the translator for speaking so rapidly," after there had been three minutes of confusion, involving a challenge to the Hebrew version, a failure by the witness to reply to O'Connor's question, and a clarification by the prosecutor. Half an hour later, the presiding judge himself asked the new court interpreter working into Hebrew to slow down. Clearly, in the Demjanjuk trial court it was not a requirement for consecutive interpreters to reproduce attorneys' speed of delivery. When working in the simultaneous mode, however, in the case of the interpreters working into English, there was no choice. The Israeli member of the defense team was reprimanded by the bench on a number of occasions for extra-rapid delivery, which at times deprived his American colleagues of the ability to follow his points in full. The following quotation conveys O'Connor's distress, unable to follow the arguments of his Hebrew-speaking fellow defense counsel Yoram Sheftel, whether because of inadequate interpretation or because of the interpreter's matching ultra-fast pace of delivery.

> I can't understand Mr. Sheftel . . . You have repeatedly asked Mr. Sheftel to slow his pace . . . I have little or no understanding of what Mr. Sheftel said . . . Perhaps I misunderstood Mr. Sheftel's response with all the rapidity . . . (June 29, 1987, 9:24 A.M.)

If this is the effect that an interpreter's high-speed delivery can have on a lawyer, one can imagine the effect that such difficulties might generate in a cross-examination situation if the interpreter were to reproduce not only the content, but also the speed of the original (as the rules would appear to imply by requiring conservation of speaker style).[15] There were, indeed, occasions at the Demjanjuk trial when the witness asked the court interpreter to speak more slowly. The bench had limited ability to keep such speeding (by lawyer or interpreter) in check. In acknowledgment of this fact, once the presiding judge even

15. R. Dueñas González, "Rate of Speech," p. 482.

observed in despair, "כמה פעמים אפשר להעיר?!" [How many times can one comment?] (June 29, 1987, 10:35 A.M.), stating, 20 minutes later, that he had instructed the interpreters "to translate as much" as they could (June 29, 1987 10:55 A.M.). Shortly after the session in question, the American lead defense lawyer was fired by his client and replaced by his Israeli colleague. Against this background, it may even be hypothesized that Yoram Sheftel's excessive speed of delivery in Hebrew was a deliberate tactic on his part, to effectively disempower his American colleagues by making complete and accurate English interpretation impossible.

Even when the interpreter was able to keep pace with a rapid-fire speaker, the client of the interpreted version was not necessarily able to follow, as in the following example.

> Defense lawyer: If you could possibly speak more slowly . . . it's extremely difficult . . . so fast that she can't capture your words . . . The translator is speaking so fast . . . If I cannot understand the interpreter. (April 8, 1987, 8:30 A.M.)

Despite the impression given by O'Connor, in this particular case the interpreter did indeed render in full everything the speaker said. For an interpreter to achieve the tour de force of providing a complete and accurate version of the rapid original, only to elicit the despairing reaction from the lawyer client: "That was so fast I could not follow" (April 1, 1987, 6:27 P.M.), was to experience a frustrating no-win situation.

CONCLUSIONS

It has been asserted that "gatekeepers who manage the translation process control the flow of information to some degree and have significant power to manipulate channels of communication" (O'Barr & O'Barr, 1976, p. 22). The behavior of the main court interpreter in the Demjanjuk trial would certainly seem to confirm this statement. Yet the reasons for her manipulative behavior are clearly not that she was unscrupulous, incompetent, irresponsible, lazy, or unaware of what she was doing, nor by any stretch of the imagination unethical. Rather, at times she deliberately adjusted her renderings pursuant to instructions from the bench, to whom she saw herself as ultimately responsible, or requests from the witness who was being questioned through the medium of her interpretation. The interpreter's behavior showed that she was not acting as a conduit or a machine (see Morris, 1999, p. 8), but was trying to contribute to the communication process taking place in the courtroom as effectively as she could, at times balancing conflicting demands and expectations, some overt and some unspoken.

The examples discussed in this paper have related mainly to the main (English to Hebrew) court interpreter at the Demjanjuk trial, who worked in the consecutive mode. A different and, on the whole, more limited range of options was available to the other interpreters using different methods of interpretation (simultaneous or whispering). There was also considerable variation in the other participants' attitudes to these additional interpreters, who were treated with far less deference, courtesy, and attention than the main court interpreter. It may therefore be hypothesized that interpersonal dynamics were responsible for a certain amount of the latitude allowed to and/or exercised by the interpreter in question. To that extent, duplicity—in both senses—may be said to have existed between bench and interpreter, creating a dynamic which put the latter firmly in charge of an important part of the interpreting process and, indirectly, of the legal process itself (albeit subject to the ultimate control of the bench).

Although the complexity of the interpreting arrangements at the Demjanjuk trial may have been unusual, the situations identified and analyzed in this paper can occur in any forensic setting. Sometimes the interpreter is specifically empowered to take control of the situation; at other times, efforts are made to banish court interpreters to the position of a "mere cypher" (*R. v. Attard,* 1958, p. 91).[16] The difference lies in the dynamic imposed by the authority figures in the proceedings, sometimes sharing or delegating their own power to the interpreter. It is unlikely that this situation will be changed however many rules or codes of practice are issued, unless judicial attitudes and the status of the interpreter change concomitantly.

16. In the 1958 English case of *Attard*, barrister Christmas Humphrey argued (unsuccessfully) that "interpreters are in a different position from that of police officers; they are impartial, mere cyphers, and are not expected to take an intelligent interest in the proceedings."

REFERENCES

Berk-Seligson, S. (1999). The impact of court interpreting on the coerciveness of leading questions. *Forensic Linguistics, 6* (1), 30–56.

Colin, J. & Morris, R. (1996). *Interpreters and the legal process.* Winchester, UK: Waterside Press.

Cronin, M. (2002). The Empire talks back: Orality, heteronomy and the cultural turn in interpreting studies. In F. Pöchhacker and M. Shlesinger (Eds.), *The interpreting studies reader* (pp. 386–397). London: Routledge.

Gonzáles, R. D., Vásquez, V., & Mikkelson, H. (1991). *Fundamentals of court interpretation.* Durham, NC: Carolina Academic Press.

Harris, B. (1981). Observations on a cause célèbre: court interpreting at the Lischka trial. In R. Roberts (Ed.), *L'interprétation auprès des tribunaux* (pp. 189–202). Ottawa: University of Ottawa Press.

Herbert, J. (1952). *The interpreter's handbook—How to become a conference interpreter.* Geneva: Librairie de l'Université.

Loftus, E. F., & Palmer, J. C. (1974). Reconstruction of automobile destruction: An example of the interaction between language and memory. *Journal of Verbal Learning and Verbal Behavior 13* (5), 585–589.

Morris, R. (1989a). *The impact of court interpretation on legal proceedings.* Unpublished master's thesis, Hebrew University of Jerusalem.

Morris, R. (1989b). Court interpretation and the record of legal proceedings: Eichmann v. Demjanjuk. *Parallèles, Cahiers de l'Ecole de Traduction et d'Interprétation 11*, 9–28.

Morris, R. (1993). *Images of the interpreter: A study of language-switching in the legal process.* Unpublished PhD thesis, Lancaster University. Available at http://RuthMorris13.googlepages.com/home.

Morris, R. (1995). The moral dilemmas of court interpreting. *The Translator 1* (1), 25–46. Available at http://RuthMorris13.googlepages.com/home.

Morris, R. (1999). The gum syndrome: predicaments in court interpreting. *Forensic Linguistics 6* (1), 6–29. Available at http://RuthMorris13.googlepages.com/home.

Morris, R. (2001). Eichmann vs. Demjanjuk: or Plus ç'est la même chose, plus ça change: The Eichmann and Demjanjuk Trials: A comparison. Paper presented at AIIC Court Interpreting Seminar, The Hague, July 2001. Available at http://RuthMorris13.googlepages.com/home.

O'Barr, W., & O'Barr, J. F. (Eds.). (1976). *Language and politics.* The Hague: Mouton.

Pym, A. (1999). Nicole slapped Michelle—Interpreters at the O. J. Simpson trial. *The Translator 5* (2), 265–283.

Shlesinger, M. (1991). Interpreter latitude vs. due process. Simultaneous and consecutive interpretation in multilingual trials. In S. Tirkkonen-Condit

(Ed.), *Empirical research in translation and intercultural studies* (pp. 147–155). Tübingen: Gunter Narr.
Walker, A. G. (1986). The verbatim record: The myth and the reality. In S. Fisher & A. D. Todd (Eds.), *Discourse and institutional authority: Medicine, education, and law* (pp. 205–222). Norwood, NJ: Ablex.

CASES CITED

Dies v. British and International Mining and Finance Corporation Ltd., 1 K.B. 724 (1939).
Hernandez v. New York, 114 L.Ed. 2d 395, 111 S. Ct. (1991).
In re Trepca Mines Ltd., 1 W.L.R. 24 (1960).
Rajnowski v. Detroit, B.C. & A.R. Co., 41 N.W. 849 (1889).
R. v. Attard, 43 Cr.App.R. 90 (1958).
Schnier v. People, 23 Ill. 11 (1859).
State of Israel v. Ivan (John) Demjanjuk, Criminal Case No. 373/86 (1987).

Interpreting in Asylum Appeal Hearings:

Roles and Norms Revisited

Waltraud Kolb and Franz Pöchhacker

The involvement of interpreters in legal proceedings with speakers of other languages has a long history, as illustrated by the sixteenth-century laws regulating judicial interpreting in the Spanish colonies. Though it received relatively little attention as a field of practice and research until the 1980s, interpreting in legal settings has since emerged as one of the major domains of the profession and of academic study. While this is true for the spoken and signed language modalities alike, the study presented here addresses a setting that is almost exclusively the domain of spoken-language interpreters.

With the exception of international tribunals, legal interpreting is typically set in a particular national context and thus constrained by a specific judicial framework and legal tradition. The resulting diversity of practices is a difficult challenge to efforts at international harmonization (e.g., Hertog, 2003), but also a rewarding one for researchers interested in the role of interpreters in the institutional search for truth and justice. This challenge is all the more extensive given the diversity of settings, ranging from police interrogations and client-lawyer consultations to administrative hearings and judicial proceedings in open court. The present study investigates legal interpreting in one of these diverse settings within a given national context, that is, asylum hearings in Austria. What is more, we focus on a particular phase in the asylum process, the appellate level, arguably the crucial one for determining an applicant's refugee status.

Given the importance of context, in its sociocultural and legal as well as institutional and situational dimensions, we begin with a brief sketch of the refugee status determination process in Austria, with particular emphasis on the appellate level. We will then review some of the main research issues and findings for interpreting in asylum hearings in general, and for first-instance proceedings in Austria in particular, before introducing our empirical study and the specific topics addressed in this paper, namely (1) the interpreter's role and participation status, and (2) the translational norms reflected in the interpreter's renderings.

UNIVERSAL RIGHT—LOCAL PRACTICE

The right to seek asylum from persecution in other countries is enshrined in the Universal Declaration of Human Rights and regulated under international law by the Geneva Convention Relating to the Status of Refugees, adopted by the United Nations in 1951, as well as the 1967 Protocol to the Convention and other international agreements. According to these fundamental legal instruments, refugee status is to be granted to individuals who have left their home country "owing to a well-founded fear of being persecuted for reasons of race, religion, nationality, membership of a particular social group or political opinion" (Art. 1, A [2]).

Notwithstanding this international legal basis and consistent efforts at establishing standard practices for refugee status determination proceedings by the United Nations High Commissioner for Refugees (UNHCR), it is up to the individual signatory states to create a legal framework and institutional structures and procedures for conducting this process under national law. Not surprisingly, national legislative arrangements exhibit considerable differences, and the role and status of interpreters in the proceedings may vary accordingly. What seems to be a common feature of the asylum process in most jurisdictions, though, is the two-tier structure typical of the legal process in general. In other words, there is a first instance or basic level at which proceedings take place in the form of asylum interviews and are concluded either by a positive or negative decision on the claim for refugee status or similar protection (non-refoulement). Applicants have the right to appeal against a negative decision, and such appeals are usually heard by a court-like institution, such as the Immigration Appeals Authority in the United Kingdom or the Permanent Commission of Appeal for Refugees in Belgium (cf., Maryns, 2006). Whereas in Germany, for instance, appeals against decisions of the first-instance asylum authority are dealt with in regular trials before a district administrative court (cf., Reischl, 2001), the Austrian system currently involves a special quasi-judicial authority, the Independent Federal Asylum Review Board (IFARB; *Unabhängiger*

Bundesasylsenat—UBAS), created in 1997 to relieve the country's Administrative Court of hearing appeals against first-instance decisions.

Whereas the Austrian first-instance authority, the Federal Asylum Office (*Bundesasylamt*), created in 1992, is staffed mainly by specially trained police officers and reports to the Ministry of the Interior, the forty-some IFARB members are appointed for life by the Austrian president and enjoy the same degree of independence as judges. While technically an administrative authority under the aegis of the Interior Ministry and thus subject to review by the Administrative Court on matters of procedure, the IFARB has many features of a judicial body that distinguish its members and its proceedings from those of the first-instance asylum authority (cf., Krainz & Wintersberger, 2006).

Since the procedural language of all Austrian public authorities is German, and since applicants for asylum, as a rule, do not have a sufficient command of that language, interpreters are an indispensable part of the entire asylum process. Applicants' right to an interpreter as laid down in the European Convention on Human Rights is mandated by the Austrian Code of Administrative Procedure in Section 39a, which applies only to oral proceedings between the authority and the parties (cf., Maurer-Kober, 2006, p. 19). However, non-German speaking parties' right to interpreting services free of charge does not imply the right to an interpreter for their native language. Rather, interpreting may be, and frequently is, offered in another language of which the applicant has a sufficient understanding and active command. Typical examples are the use of Russian for asylum seekers from Chechnya and the use of English for claimants from anglophone African countries, as in the corpus under study. (On the critical issue of imposed language choice, see Maryns, 2006, chap. 2.) Unlike in Germany, applicants for asylum may not supply an interpreter of their choosing at their own expense, but they do have the right to reject an interpreter hired by the authority if there is evidence of bias or lack of qualification.

The interpreter for a given appeal hearing is contracted by the IFARB member assigned to the case, who will conduct the hearing and issue the decision as the sole adjudicator. Interpreters are drawn from an internal list that includes court-certified interpreters as well as others who have offered their services to the authority. Court-certified status is not a prerequisite, and some of the more than 60 languages used in hearings before the IFARB are so exotic in the Austrian context that it is sometimes difficult to find anyone to serve as an interpreter.

RESEARCH ISSUES

The availability of qualified interpreters for asylum hearings is one of the most critical issues in this field and has been discussed from the legal as well as the linguistic point of view (e.g., Anker, 1991; Kälin, 1986; Monnier, 1995). Aside from this major organizational and training challenge, the overriding theme in research on interpreting in the asylum process appears to be the interpreter's role, with particular emphasis on the extent to which s/he may or should go beyond the task of relaying the primary participants' utterances and take more active responsibility for the achievement of cross-cultural understanding. The most radical proposal in this regard was introduced to the translation studies community by Robert Barsky (1996), who concluded from his interview-based study of Canadian Convention refugee hearings that the interpreter should act as an "intercultural agent," improving the asylum seekers' chances of receiving a fair hearing by better articulating their claims, filling in cultural gaps, and compensating for errors of judgment.

In a questionnaire-based survey among interpreters serving the Refugee Status Appeals Authority in New Zealand, Sabine Fenton (2004) sought to gauge the level of practitioners' support for Barsky's (1996) "extreme demands." Though she found that most of her 35 respondents expressed sympathy for the disadvantaged position of the asylum seekers in the face of interviewers' often cold and even hostile questioning style, they were unanimous in endorsing the "accurate interpreting" norm and preferring to be "as invisible and unobtrusive as possible" (Fenton, 2004, p. 268).

Taking a more ethnographic as well as a macro-sociological approach, Moira Inghilleri (2003, 2005) concluded from her study of the asylum application system in the United Kingdom that there were two distinct concepts of interpreting, namely "linguistic" and "community" interpreting, and that these differing approaches in using interpreters "can lead to substantial confusion about their role both among interpreters themselves and those who use their services" (2003, p. 1).

Methodologically, none of the authors cited above studied role-related claims by analyzing authentic corpora of interpreter-mediated discourse. While there have been a number of studies on asylum hearings by researchers in such fields as conversation and institutional discourse analysis (e.g., Maryns, 2006; Reischl, 2001) and sociology (e.g., Scheffer, 2001), very little research based on discourse data has been carried out in the field of translation and interpreting studies. Aside from communication scholar and interpreter Cecilia Wadensjö (1998), who drew, inter alia, on interactional sociolinguistics to study dialogue interpreting in immigration interviews, the most extensive discourse-based work to date in translation studies is that of Sonja Pöllabauer (2004, 2005). In her study of first-instance asylum hearings in Graz, Austria, she analyzed a corpus of 20 audio-recorded and fully transcribed asylum interviews conducted by three different officials with English-speaking applicants from four African countries. Drawing on translation theory, critical discourse analysis, and linguistic pragmatics, Pöllabauer examined the performance of three interpreters with regard to their role performance, their positioning in the primary parties' asymmetrical power relation, and their adherence to professional norms. On the whole, she finds "highly discrepant behaviour which seems to be determined mainly by the officers' expectations" (Pöllabauer, 2004, pp. 174–175) and observes that the interpreters, far from being "invisible" and neutral, intervene in a number of ways. Rather than serving as intercultural agents as suggested by Barsky (1996), the interpreters in Pöllabauer's study assume the role of "auxiliary police officers" whose loyalty ultimately lies with the adjudicating officials. Thus, interpreters were found to omit "irrelevant" information and admonish the asylum seekers to provide "concrete" answers; to engage in "internal rounds of talk" that remained untranslated for the other party; and to verbally ally with the officials by using the first person plural to refer to the adjudicator–interpreter team.

For obvious reasons, Pöllabauer's groundbreaking discourse-based study of asylum hearings suggests itself as a point of departure for the study reported here. For one, the findings sketched out above relate only to first-instance proceedings and cannot be generalized to the Austrian refugee status determination process as a whole. As described earlier, interviewing (and adjudicating) officials in first-instance hearings mostly have a background as police officers rather than a full-scale legal education. Moreover, appeal hearings, which are quasi-judicial proceedings involving two parties, could be assumed to differ from first-instance interviews with regard to organizational arrangements, interactional structure, and discursive functions. Indeed, findings from a survey by Maurer-Kober (2004) among IFARB members suggest that nearly half of the 30 respondents are "often" confronted with appellants complaining about communication difficulties with the interpreter(s) in their first-instance interview. With good reason, then, IFARB members were found to take special care in selecting interpreters for their hearings. Asked about their re-hiring criteria, for instance, the IFARB members in Maurer-Kober's survey gave special attention to such criteria as "strictly neutral behavior" and "smooth facilitation of communication" (each rated "very important" by nearly three-quarters of the respondents on a four-point scale from "very important" to "unimportant"). By the same token, an overwhelming majority of IFARB members expect interpreters to serve as "neutral linguistic mediators" rather than "auxiliaries to the adjudicator" or "cultural mediators." Moreover, IFARB members do not give interpreters license to "omit irrelevant information in order to save time," and a clear majority of them (70%) would not permit the interpreter to "clarify vague responses by asking follow-up questions." Most IFARB members feel that their expectations are met by the interpreters' actual performance. Asked about their level of satisfaction with the quality of interpreting, 72% of the respondents said that they were "very satisfied" as opposed to "somewhat satisfied" (28%) or "not satisfied" (0%).

Given this rich and differentiated body of empirical findings on the role and task of interpreters in the Austrian asylum process, our study takes a two-pronged approach; that is, examining asylum hearings at the appellate level for similarities and differences with regard to Pöllabauer's findings (inter alia, on role behavior and professional norms), and comparing actual practices in interpreter-mediated appeal hearings to adjudicators' expectations and perceptions of interpreters and their role(s).

METHOD AND DATA

Our fieldwork on interpreting practices in asylum hearings at the IFARB was conceived as an ethnographic study with a focus on the analysis of audio-recorded hearings.[1] Given our own linguistic qualifications and the composition of Pöllabauer's corpus, the scope of our project was limited to asylum review hearings involving English-speaking appellants, more precisely, to cases of asylum seekers from anglophone African countries.

1. This project, initiated by the second author, was supported by the University of Vienna with a grant (F009-G) to the first author. This financial assistance is gratefully acknowledged.

After the IFARB chairman had endorsed our study proposal and granted us access to the institution for data collection, five IFARB members (three women, two men) agreed to take part in the study. Following advance notice of the date and time of hearings, we participated as observers and brought a digital tape recorder (Sony TCD-D8) fitted with an external stereo microphone to record the hearings. While in most cases the interpreters had been informed in advance by the official that the hearing would be taped for research purposes, the asylum seekers were approached before the hearing in the waiting area and asked for their permission after a brief explanation of the aims and methods of our study. They were told, in particular, that all personal data would remain anonymous and that the study had no bearing whatsoever on the outcome of their cases. Having agreed to the recording, they received detailed information about the project in writing (in English) and were expressly advised that they could revoke their permission at any time during or after the hearing. Permission to record was granted in all cases but one.[2]

A total of 14 hearings conducted by the five adjudicators and involving seven different interpreters (five women, two men) were recorded between October 2005 and October 2006, amounting to a total duration of 25 hours. On average, hearings lasted about 100 minutes, ranging from 26 minutes to 3.5 hours. The sample of interpreters exhibited a range of professional qualifications and experience. The majority had MA-level training in interpreting and considerable professional experience, and most were court-certified interpreters. Out of the 14 asylum seekers in the study, 12 came from Nigeria and 1 each from Gambia and Zimbabwe.

The recordings on digital audio tape were converted into digital audio files and transcribed orthographically using standard word-processing and media-player software. In addition to the corpus of audio-recordings and transcriptions, our data also include fieldnotes from participant observation and informal interviews.

ANALYSIS

Our analytical approach was informed by the tenets of functionalist translation theory, or skopos theory, as presented, for instance, in Nord

2. We would like to express our sincere thanks to the asylum seekers and interpreters for their permission to be recorded for this study, and in particular to the IFARB members who granted us access to their hearings.

(1997). Thus, our understanding of the data was guided by our concern with the institutional purpose of the communicative event and with the interaction and the relevant characteristics of the individual participants. Moreover, our analysis draws on concepts of interaction and discourse analysis as applied by Wadensjö (1998).

Out of the many interesting observations to be gleaned from a close study of this rich corpus of data, we have selected the following two aspects for presentation in this paper: (1) the role(s) and participation status of the interpreter and the adjudicating official working as an ad hoc team; and (2) the translational norms reflected in the interpreter's renderings, in particular the use of the speaker's "I" (first person) as well as the classic standards of accuracy and completeness.

Situational Context and Structure

Unlike first-instance asylum hearings, appellate proceedings at the IFARB involve two parties, the asylum seeker and the Federal Asylum Office, whose negative decision is being challenged. In practice, the first-instance authority is not represented in these hearings. Therefore, the constellation of interactants normally includes the adjudicating official, the asylum seeker, the interpreter, and the recording clerk. Persons of the asylum seekers' confidence and other observers are also admitted to these public hearings. Although the proceedings are of a similar nature as those in a courtroom, the general setup is considerably less formal. The hearings usually take place in plain, medium-sized rooms furnished with a small number of chairs arranged around a set of joined-up tables. There is no raised seating position for the adjudicator and no special bench for the appellant, nor do the representatives of the institution appear in formal attire such as robes or gowns. The recording clerk sits next to the adjudicator in front of a computer screen; the appellant is usually seated in a chair roughly facing the official, and the interpreter usually takes up a position between the two primary interactants.

Although it is possible for the adjudicating official to decide a case only on the basis of the documents on file, most appeals involve a hearing in which the asylum seeker is given another opportunity to present his or her claim. Hearings are conducted by the IFARB member assigned to the case and typically include the following seven stages: (1) verification of personal data and current address; (2) procedural information and instruction; (3) summary of the facts of the case; (4) taking of evidence, that is, interviewing and questioning; (5) presentation of country-related information; (6) announcement that the decision will be issued in writing; and (7) sight translation into English and signing of the written record.

The core of the hearing is stage four, the interview, in which the asylum seeker is asked about his or her reasons for leaving the country, the circumstances of his or her life before the flight, and about his or her escape route. This leads into a round of questioning, in which the adjudicating official confronts the asylum seeker with apparent inconsistencies in his or her narrative and with discrepancies with respect to statements as recorded in the first-instance hearing. Hence, the institutional purpose of the proceedings is to establish the facts of the case and to assess the credibility of the asylum seeker and his or her story. In this, the interpreter plays a crucial and complex role, as shown in the following sections of this analysis.

Roles and Participation Status

In principle, the interactants' roles are well defined by the institutional context, that is, the adjudicating official conducts the hearing and ensures that its contents are reflected in the written record; the asylum seeker presents his or her claim and responds to the official's questions; the interpreter renders the adjudicating official's statements and questions in the language understood by the asylum seeker and the latter's utterances in the language of the proceedings; and the recording clerk types what is dictated to be entered in the record. The interpreter's normative role as commonly laid down in interpreters' codes of ethics and standards of professional practice and specifically described for the refugee status determination process (e.g., UNHCR, 1995; BMI et al., 2006) is thus limited to rendering the primary parties' utterances accurately and completely, without adding, omitting or changing anything, and using the grammatical first person of the speaker.

As demonstrated by Pöllabauer (2004, 2005) for first-instance proceedings, actual role behavior in the interaction tends to be much more complex, and a similar pattern of complexity emerges from the current study. We present examples of three types of deviations from the interpreter's normative role: verbally allying with the adjudicator, acting as co-interviewer, and co-producing the written record.

NEUTRAL AND "INVISIBLE"?

Though strongly challenged by recent scholarship (e.g. Metzger, 1999; Angelelli, 2004), the idea that interpreters are neutral between the primary parties and do not intervene on behalf of either side, is deeply entrenched, both in the interpreting community and, in particular, among users of their services, as illustrated in the expectations voiced by IFARB members in Maurer-Kober's (2004) study. And yet, as shown by Pöllabauer (2004), interpreters frequently position themselves as members of the institutional "team," for instance by adopting the first person plural to refer to the asylum seeker's interlocutor(s). The following excerpt from the corpus (Example 1) is one of many examples of such a verbal alliance forged by the interpreter's use of the "inclusive 'we'" (cf., Pöllabauer, 2004, pp. 168–169). It is taken from the central part of a hearing in which the appellant is questioned about threatening events in the course of his flight to and stay in the Nigerian city of Lagos.

EXAMPLE 1: T1H2 (34:21–34:36): **"we need to know"**

1	ADJ	Was konkret ist im Panama Hotel passiert? *What exactly happened in the Panama Hotel?*
2	INT	What exactly happened in Panama Hotel, in Lagos?
3	APP	Yea, while while I was there they attack me.
4	INT	Yes, **we need to know** exactly what happened during the attack. (→REC) Als ich dort war °° griffen sie mich an. *When I was there °° they attacked me.*

ADJ's question to elicit concrete information (1) is rendered by INT with added (though contextually available) information concerning the place. Before giving her German rendition of APP's answer, INT responds directly, as "co-principal," emphasizing the need for concrete information (4). In doing so, INT indicates to APP that his answer is not yet satisfactory, that is, not specific enough, and the opening part of her utterance ("Yes") clearly implies "yes, but" (see also Example 2 below). INT thus assumes responsibility for the institutional purpose of the hearing, which is to establish concrete facts about the asylum claim. Nevertheless, INT does not ask a follow-up question but proceeds to render APP's answer in German, pausing after the first clause as REC is typing her interpretation into the record.

The self-initiated admonition by INT in Example 1 (4) points to a tendency of interpreters to take on tasks that go beyond their normative role.

Some interpreters in our study even assume an active "co-interviewer" role, as shown in the following section.

THE INTERPRETER AS CO-INTERVIEWER

As observed by Scheffer (2001) and also documented in Pöllabauer's corpus, interpreters in asylum hearings tend to take on an active interviewing role to elicit further or more specific information. The extent to which they may do so, however, depends on the official conducting the hearing. While some adjudicators appear to be happy with interpreters conducting sub-hearings of varying length, others would not give up their prerogative to ask the questions, as illustrated in the following examples.

The interpreter in Example 2 is very active also in the sense of cutting in before the previous utterance has been completed, as seen in turns 2, 6, and 15. Similar to his colleague in Example 1 above, he responds to an answer by APP that he considers too vague by expressing disapproval ("Yes, but") rather than rendering what APP has said (4).

EXAMPLE 2: T4H1 (06:40–07:40)

1 ADJ Welche Religion gehen Sie nach?
What religion do you practice?
2 INT What What is your religion, your faith?
3 APP Christian.
4 INT Yes, but-
5 APP Church was- is a Pentecostal church.
6 INT Episcopal, or . . . . Pentecostal?
7 APP Yeah.
8 INT Also, ə Ch- Ich bin Christin und gehöre einer- der Pfingstkirche *So, ə Ch- I am a Christian and belong to a- the Pentecostal church-*
—(→ADJ) ich glaub das is' ka anerkannte bei uns.
I think that's not a recognized one here.
9 ADJ Mhm. (? ?)
10 INT Ja, Pentecostal.
Yes, Pentecostal.
11 ADJ (→REC) Pfingst— *Pentecost-*
12 INT Pfingstkirche.
Pentecostal church.
13 ADJ (→REC) Pfingst- °° Pfingstkirche an. °° °° °° °° °° °° °°
Pentecost- °° to a Pentecostal church.
(→APP) Und haben Sie Ihre Religion ausgeübt?
And did you practice your religion?

14 INT Did you practice that religion?
15 APP Yeah, I was a Christian! And I go to church.
16 INT Yes, but but- look, there are many Christians who never go to ch- You went to church?
17 APP Yes.
18 INT Ich bin in die Kirche gegangen.
I went to church.
19 ADJ (→REC) Ich bin in die Kirche gegangen. °° °° °° °° °° °°
I went to church.
(→INT) Darf ich Sie nur ersuchen, solche Fragen nicht zu stellen, gell.
May I just ask you not to put such questions, okay?

While INT's initiative (4) makes APP understand that some specification is needed (5), INT interrupts her with an explicit prompt (6) before he registers APP's answer, which he renders in German (8) after a brief clarification turn (6, 7). Before completing his rendition, however, INT volunteers a comment to ADJ about the denomination in question. APP's answer is subsequently recorded upon repeated dictation by ADJ (11, 13), who then proceeds to ask a follow-up question about APP's religious practice (13). As in the earlier part of this sequence, INT reacts immediately to APP's—here somewhat indignant—response, expressing disapproval with the seemingly insufficient answer ("Yes, but but-") and venturing into some extensive reasoning before taking note of the second part of her reply (16). Again, a clarification turn precedes INT's German rendition (18), which is repeated by ADJ for inclusion in the record. When this has been accomplished by REC during a six-second pause, ADJ finally turns to INT, a court-certified interpreter with many years of experience in legal settings with whom she is working for the first time, and politely requests him not to ask questions on his own initiative (19).

In contrast to this particular IFARB member's preference for a more restricted role of the interpreter in the interviewing process, other adjudicating officials in our study showed fewer qualms about letting the interpreters conduct their own sub-hearings with the asylum seekers. The following example is a particularly striking case of such interpreter-led interviewing. After ADJ's standard question as to whether APP had been going to school or working before leaving his home country (1), INT proceeds to elicit APP's complete educational background—and much more.

EXAMPLE 3: T1H1 (06:20–07:39): **"How many years? . . . Did you finish?"**

1	ADJ	Haben Sie einen Beruf ausgeübt? Oder waren Sie in einer Ausbildung? *Were you working? Or were you attending school?*
2	INT	Did you work? Or did you study?
3	APP	Yeah, I went to primary school at the age of seven,
4	INT	Mhm.
5	APP	so I finished up primary school for six years, so-
6	INT	Ich- Ich trat mit sieben Jahren in die Grundschule ein, °° °° °° °° °° °° absolvierte diese für sechs Jahre °° *I- I started primary school at the age of seven, attended this school for six years °°* (→APP) So six years of primary school?
7	APP	Yeah, so after one year for my- for the written result then I proceeded to secondary school.
8	INT	Nach einem Jahr °° Warten °° kam ich *After one year °° of waiting °° I was sent*
9	APP	Then-
10	INT	in die Sekundarschule. (→APP) **How many years of secondary school?** *to secondary school.*
11	APP	Two years, only two years.
12	ADJ	(→REC) in die Sekundarschule °° °° °° °° °° Sekund- so wie Sekund, Sekundar *to secondary school second- like second, secondary*
13	REC	Mhm.
14	INT	**Did you finish secondary school?**
15	APP	No I didn't finish.
16	INT	Ich besuchte die Sekundarschule für zwei Jahre °° °° °° °° °° °° ° und schloss sie °° aber nicht ab. °° *I attended secondary school for two years but did not finish it.* (→APP) So two years of secondary school, and then?

APP does not understand ADJ's question as referring to the time just before his flight, but starts to recount his formal education from primary school onwards (3). INT is aware that APP's statement about starting school at age seven is not what ADJ is after; rather than translating it, INT signals APP to continue ("Mhm."). Only when complete information about primary schooling has become available (5), does she cut in to offer her German rendition (5). The question she then addresses to APP might appear like a request for confirmation; in fact, though, it exemplifies this interpreter's key strategy in eliciting APP's account. Using an intonation contour that signals recapitulation as well as an invitation to continue, INT moves the interview forward without the need for ADJ to intervene. Indeed, the latter's role appears to be limited to supervising REC's typing of INT's renditions, at times repeating parts of them and assisting REC in case of orthographic doubts (12).

Aside from the more covert tactic of pseudo-confirmation prompts, INT also resorts to explicit direct questions in a co-interviewer capacity, as seen in turns 10 and 14. Once she has thus gathered sufficient information, INT formulates her German rendition, pausing for REC in keeping with her typing speed. A third prompting strategy, which is actually a combination of the other two, is seen at the end of turn 16, where INT recapitulates APP's previous statement ("two years of secondary school") and then adds an explicit prompt for him to continue ("and then?"). A variation on the latter, used frequently by the interpreter whose active role was illustrated in Example 2 is the use of the direct prompt "Go on, please!" to elicit APP's narrative. As shown in Example 5(2) another, less imperative technique is the use of "Alright?"

What is most exceptional about the previous excerpt presented to illustrate the interpreter's technique of conducting independent sub-hearings, is that it represents only a fraction of the interview in which INT adopts the same co-principal role throughout. Whereas the (incomplete) interview sequence about APP's education (Example 3 lasts barely one-and-a-half minutes), the evidence-gathering stage of that hearing, which is essentially conducted by the interpreter as interviewer, lasts more than three-quarters of an hour. ADJ only takes charge of the hearing again when APP's story of flight has been finished.

In addition to these interpreters' extraordinarily active role as co-interviewers, they also play a crucial part in the production of the written record—a function that has so far received little, if any, attention in research on interpreting in legal settings.

INTERPRETING FOR THE RECORD

Whereas the interpreter's normative role is generally focused on the task of accurately and completely "relaying" (translating) the primary parties' spoken (or signed) utterances as well as on some degree of managing or "coordinating" the flow of discourse (cf., Roy, 2000; Wadensjö,

1998), the interpreting practices observed in hearings at the IFARB suggest a third dimension of the interpreter's task in this type of event. As pointed out by Scheffer (2001) and Pöllabauer (2005), interpreters are expected to formulate their translations of asylum seekers' statements in such a way that they can be entered directly into the record. These authors generally assume, however, that responsibility for the record, in both principle and practice, rests with the adjudicating official, who would repeat (or rephrase) the interpreter's spoken output and dictate it for typing. While there can be no doubt about the adjudicator's full legal accountability for the record, it is altogether surprising to what extent the interpreters in our study become involved in the production of the record.

It is not possible in the scope of this paper to explore all the various mechanisms—and consequences—of the interpreters' co-production of the record, and we will present only one of many examples in the corpus to make our point. In the following excerpt (Example 4), INT is seen dictating her output with well-timed pauses for REC to finish her typing—and even complete with instructions for punctuation.

EXAMPLE 4: T1H1 (19:22–19:48): ***"colon, quotation mark"***

1 APP So when he rushed to me I I- when he rushed to the office I w- I was
sur- surprised a- what happened? what happened? <u>He said-</u>

2 INT <u>Ich war sehr</u>
überrascht, °° als er hereingestürmt kam °° °° °° °° °° °° °° und fragte °°
°° °° **Doppelpunkt, Anführungszeichen** °° °° Was ist denn passiert?
Was ist passiert? *I was very*
surprised, when he came storming in and asked
colon, quotation mark *But what happened?*
What happened?
(→APP) Alright?

APP's narration of a shocking message being delivered to him in his office (1) is full of hesitation and false starts. Not surprisingly, no trace of these is left in INT's—otherwise rather "close"—German rendition. APP's repetition ("what happened") is retained in the interpretation for dramatic effect (2), but the latter is obviously ruined for the listener by INT's indication of the punctuation marks required (in German) to indicate direct speech.

More so than the other examples (with the exception of Example 3, involving the same interpreter), Example 4 also includes clear evidence that the interpreter's German delivery is adapted to REC's typing speed and that the target text here is not so much an oral rendering of a spoken utterance than a dictation of what is to be scripted—a finding that corroborates Hale's (2004) results for interpreters' treatment of style.

Professional Norms

The role-related phenomena described earlier mainly concern what is done in the interaction, and by whom. The following sections, on the other hand, address the question of how it is done, with special reference, of course, to the performance of the interpreters.

As defined by Chesterman (1993, p. 8), "[p]rofessional norms are the norms constituted by competent professional behaviour." These are subordinate to what he calls "expectancy norms," which are the correctness notions brought to bear on translational output by the users or addressees of the target text. Admittedly, it is not always easy to make a clear-cut distinction between the interpreter's professional role (which implies norm-guided behavior) and professional or performance norms (which would be founded on the adoption of a particular role). This conceptual complexity notwithstanding, the focus on translational norms, particularly of the textual-linguistic kind, helps foreground features of interpreting performance that are often cited as the crucial standards of professional interpreting. Summarized by Harris (1990, p. 118) as the "true interpreter norm," these will be examined here with regard to the expectation of accuracy and completeness as well as the professional interpreting norm that "the interpreter speaks in the first person" (Harris, p. 115).

USE OF FIRST PERSON

Without going into the more elaborate conceptual framework proposed by Bot (2005), which accounts for the use of reporting verbs as well as the "perspective of person," there are two basic options for the interpreter's pronoun use in rendering utterances in which speakers make reference to themselves. One is to adopt the grammatical first person as used by the speaker, and the other is to reserve the first person for the interpreter's own 'I' and refer to the speaker in the third person, thus assuming the footing of principal, with responsibility for the content and form of the message. In the former case, adopting the much-cited conduit role, interpreters are only (re-)formulating others' talk and remain without a speaker perspective of their own (i.e., invisible) whereas in the latter they speak as a third party to one primary participant about another. The following excerpt, taken from the very beginning of a hearing, illustrates the classic first-person interpreting approach (cf. also Diriker, 2004).

EXAMPLE 5: T5H1 (00:11–00:24)

1 ADJ Mein Name ist VORNAME NACHNAME, ich bin das für Ihr Berufungsverfahren hier zuständige Senatsmitglied des Unabhängigen Bundesasylsenates.
My name is FIRST NAME SURNAME, I am the member of the Independent Federal Asylum Review Board in charge of your appeal proceedings.

2 INT My name is Doctor SURNAME. I am the member of the Senate dealing with your appeal proceedings.

As regards pronoun use, INT strictly maintains the speaker perspective of ADJ ("My name," "I am"). In other respects, more relevant to the subsections below, there are interesting deviations, such as the addition of ADJ's academic degree before (only) the surname (which would be common practice in German more so than in English) and the omission of the institution's official name, which reduces ADJ's affiliation to "member of the Senate."

Example 6, which is again an excerpt from an early stage of the proceedings, illustrates the opposite approach, adopted by the vast majority of the interpreters in our study.

EXAMPLE 6: T6H1 (04:12–04:24)

1 ADJ Gut. Ich möchte Ihnen nun ganz kurz ə zeigen, welche Art von Unterlagen wir in Ihrem Akt haben.
Alright. I would now like to show you briefly what kind of documents we have in your file.

2 INT Mhm. The Chairman of the Asylum Board will now just go through all the documents that he has, that you have presented.

Whereas ADJ uses the direct form of address ("*I*" → "*you*") in explaining to APP that he is about to enter into stage 3 of the hearing, that is, summarizing the case based on the documents on file, INT opts for a change of speaker perspective and renders the statement in "indirect translation" (Bot, 2005). This creates the need to designate ADJ in his official capacity. However, INT's terminological choice ("Chairman of the Asylum Board") is incorrect; the IFARB has dozens of individual "members" serving as adjudicators, but only one "Chairperson" for the institution as such.

No less problematic is INT's statement regarding the documents in APP's file, not all of which have been "presented" by APP. This applies in particular to the written record of the first-instance proceedings, which serves as critical evidence in ADJ's endeavor to probe APP's credibility. But again, this is not a matter of pronoun use but one of accuracy, as dealt with in the following section.

ACCURACY

While it is difficult at the textual-discursive level to separate accuracy and completeness, the former is most easily applied with reference to smaller elements of discourse, as in lexical and terminological accuracy. Whereas questions of institutional terminology should hardly prove intractable, interpreters can never have ready-made solutions for all and any lexical contingencies arising within the interaction. But this confronts us head-on with the fraught translation-theoretical issue of fidelity (or meaning equivalence, sense consistency, etc.) that will not be expatiated on in this particular context. Rather, we will present an example of a much less subtle or debatable lexical deviation, indicating the potential for semantic distortions of the asylum seeker's statements that may end up in the written record.

In the sequence preceding the excerpt below, ADJ has just asked APP about his father's political activity and now tries to find out more about APP's own involvement.

EXAMPLE 7: T6H2 (67:35–68:05)

1 ADJ Und jetzt er selbst?
And now he himself?

2 INT Mhm. And you personally? Did you have anything to do with his political activity?

3 APP Yeah, I was supporting, you know.

4 ADJ (→REC) Ich war ein Unterstützer.
I was a supporter.
(→APP) Können Sie mir darüber <u>etwas erzählen?</u>
Can you tell me something about that?

5 APP <u>Because everybody</u> is free when the election was coming, you can support somebody when you like, you know, any person you like.

6 INT Mhm. Es kann jeder die Partei wählen, die er will, wenn es gerade Wahlen gibt.
Mhm. Everyone can vote for the party he likes when there are elections.

7 REC (→REC) Bitte?
Sorry?

8 INT Wenn es Wahlen gibt, kann jeder die Partei wählen, die er will.
When there are elections, everyone can vote for the party he likes.

Example 7 contains a number of phenomena worth noting, such as one of the rare instances of an indirectly addressed question by ADJ (1); ADJ's direct formulation of the German rendition for the record, assuming the role of interpreter; and REC's request for repetition, addressed to INT rather than ADJ. We will, however, limit our comments to the lexical deviation in turn 6, where INT renders APP's statement about someone's right to "support" (a person) (5) as the right to "*vote for*" (a party). It is this rendering that ends up in the record, having even been repeated by INT upon REC's request. Depending on APP's age and the other facts of the case, the shift from "supporting" to "voting" might well engender contradictions that could undermine APP's credibility.

COMPLETENESS

As in the case of semantic inaccuracy, an interpreter's incomplete rendering can be detrimental to the asylum seeker's case. The following example illustrates this for an abridged translation of ADJ's questioning.

EXAMPLE 8: T5H1 (57:32–58:21)

1 ADJ Sie haben °° °° °° °° °° weder °° °° vor dem Bundesasylamt noch heute in der bisherigen Verhandlung davon gesprochen, dass man Sie mehrmals aufgefordert hat, diesen Trank zu sich zu nehmen, und Sie haben auch nicht angegeben bis dato, dass Sie irgendwann einmal davon getrunken haben. °° °° Wie erklären Sie mir diesen Widerspruch?
Neither at the Federal Asylum Office nor in today's hearing up to now have you mentioned that you were asked several times to drink that potion, and so far you also have not indicated that you ever did drink from it. How do you explain this contradiction to me?

2 INT Neither in your previous statement before the Federal Asylum Office nor today you said that you were asked to drink this potion several times, and you a- neither did you say that you drunk from it once.

Critically, in this credibility-testing stage of the hearing, ADJ confronts APP with an alleged contradiction and asks him explicitly to try and resolve it ("*How do you explain this contradiction to me?*"). While INT renders the references that allegedly contradict APP's most recent statement, she does not translate the concluding prompt for APP to explain the discrepancy. APP is merely reminded that he did not say previously what he has said now, and is thus not alerted to the threat to his credibility, nor to the need to counter it with an explanation. Similar kinds of omissions occur elsewhere in the corpus and deserve to be examined further for their impact on the course and outcome of the proceedings.

DISCUSSION AND CONCLUSION

In view of the explosive growth of the number of asylum seekers worldwide and the concomitant significance of interpreting in the refugee status determination process, the study reported here sought to investigate the challenges relating to the roles and professional norms of interpreters working in this increasingly important legal setting. With qualitative findings on Austrian first-instance proceedings (Pöllabauer, 2004, 2005) and quantitative survey results on the Austrian asylum appeals authority (Maurer-Kober, 2004) as invaluable points of departure, we studied interpreting practices at the Independent Federal Asylum Review Board (IFARB) in relation to both the role- and norm-related findings for first-instance asylum interviews and to IFARB members' expectations and preferences regarding the role performance of interpreters contracted to work with them.

Based on a close examination of our 25-hour corpus of audio-taped interviews with appellants from three anglophone African countries, we were able to gain a number of valuable insights, some of which are presented in this paper. Most importantly, the general expectation of adjudicating officials at the IFARB, that interpreters serve as "neutral linguistic mediators" rather than "auxiliaries to the adjudicator" was not borne out by our discourse-based analysis. Rather, interpreters were often found to take on tasks that go far beyond an interpreter's normative role as laid down in professional codes of ethics and standards of practice, and these extended roles are ostensibly ratified by the adjudicators in the interaction. As illustrated with excerpts from the corpus, some interpreters assume an active co-interviewer role, applying specific questioning and prompting strategies to elicit asylum seekers' narratives in internal sub-hearings.

Viewed in terms of the skopos or overall purpose of the communicative event, this practice arguably facilitates the information-gathering procedure across language barriers, especially in cases where asylum seekers' responses are vague and difficult to understand. The interpreters, who have after all been contracted by the authority, thus become agents of institutional efficiency. This phenomenon has also been described for healthcare settings, with opinions divided over whether interpreters can or should indeed be given license to act as co-diagnosticians or co-therapists. In the asylum hearings observed, the interpreter's interviewing function in, for instance, eliciting the narrative of escape is undoubtedly controversial; in some respects, though, it can be said to benefit the asylum seekers, who are assisted in telling their stories ("Then what happened?") and receive confirmation that their most recent statement has been understood and entered in the record ("So two years of secondary school, and then?"). Similarly, interpreters responding to vague answers by directly admonishing the appellant to be more specific ("Yes, but-," "We need to know exactly . . .") help elicit a detailed account, which is also what adjudicators state as the main purpose of the hearing in the introductory stage of the proceedings.

The extent to which interpreters can go beyond their normative role certainly depends on the adjudicator, and we have shown one example (Example 2) of an official curtailing the interpreter's interviewing function. In hearings involving English, the adjudicators can easily monitor and restrict such practices. In the case of other, often very exotic languages, which are typical of day-to-day practice at the IFARB, the officials would be much less able to decide which interventions to accept. It may clearly be difficult to draw the line between overeager co-interviewing and asking clarification questions that are needed to ensure proper comprehension (particularly in the case of the African English speakers in our corpus) and that are therefore indispensable for avoiding errors in the written record.

Though a major challenge and achievement in itself, providing accurate translations is by no means the interpreter's only production task. One of the most striking findings in our study is that most adjudicators expected interpreters to take on the role of co-producers of the written record. Though mentioned by Scheffer (2001) and Pöllabauer (2005), this phenomenon has not yet been demonstrated and discussed in great detail. The corpus extracts included in this paper serve to illustrate a few mechanisms and consequences of this practice, a fuller account of which will be presented in a separate publication. What is readily apparent from our examples is that interpreters assuming this function tend not only to time their renderings to accommodate the recording clerk's typing speed but also to give explicit instructions for punctuation ("colon, quotation mark"). Moreover, the interpreters cooperate directly with the recording clerk in matters of spelling and by repeating their renditions for the benefit of the typist.

The practice of interpreting directly for the record frequently involves stylistic shifts from oral to more literate renderings, as exemplified briefly in this paper. Given the critical significance of the written record as a basis for assessing an applicant's credibility and thus reaching—and justifying—the ultimate decision on the claim, the issue of the inevitable filtering process that occurs on several levels when producing the written record (cf. Maryns, 2006) requires more comprehensive analysis in future publications.

The traditional notion of interpreters' neutrality and invisibility has been challenged by recent scholarship, for interpreting in general (e.g., Angelelli, 2004; Diriker, 2004) and for asylum hearings in particular (e.g., Pöllabauer, 2004, 2005). Our data clearly corroborate this trend, as illustrated by interpreters' tendency to forge verbal alliances with the adjudicators by using the inclusive "we."

Under the broad notion of professional translational norms, we have also discussed the interpreting performances in our corpus with regard to the classic quality standards of accuracy and completeness as well as the use of the first person in professional interpreting. Our findings confirm that deviations from these norms occur in interpreting at the appellate level of asylum hearings just as they do at the first-instance level investigated by Pöllabauer. While we did not embark on a discussion of the fraught theoretical issue of translational fidelity, our examples indicate the risk of semantic distortions finding their way into the written record, and the potential impact of incomplete renderings (e.g., of an adjudicator's prompt for the appellant to explain an apparent contradiction) on the course and outcome of the proceedings.

As with any transcription-based qualitative study of this kind, the findings reported here should not be viewed as representative, neither of interpreting practices at the IFARB nor even of the work of interpreters for English in that institution or even of the working styles of the seven interpreters in our corpus. Variable situational and contextual constraints require great flexibility in problem-solving, and translational decisions that may be judged appropriate in one case may be less felicitous in another. Also, our intention in collecting and analyzing this corpus has been essentially descriptive rather than prescriptive. Even so, we hope that the institution that has granted us access to these data, the IFARB members and the interpreters they work with, and, not least, the appellants in future hearings may benefit from the reflections and discussions we hope to generate with our findings.

While our corpus is among the largest that have so far been collected and analyzed in this domain, the limitations pointed out above rather make it a (substantial) pilot study, limited to interpreting in one particular language and to one particular (Austrian) institution at the appellate level of asylum proceedings. Nevertheless, we are convinced that our findings are relevant also to hearings in other languages and national contexts, and hope that fellow interpreting researchers will carry out similar and further work on asylum hearings, thereby according this significant field of practice the attention it deserves.

REFERENCES

Angelelli, C. V. (2004). *Revisiting the interpreter's role: A study of conference, court, and medical interpreters in Canada, Mexico, and the United States*. Amsterdam: John Benjamins.

Anker, D. E. (1991). Determining asylum claims in the United States: Executive summary of an empirical study of the adjudication of asylum claims before the Immigration Court. In H. Adelman (Ed.), *Refugee policy: Canada and the United States* (pp. 268–281). Toronto: York Lanes Press.

Barsky, R. F. (1996). The interpreter as intercultural agent in Convention refugee hearings. *The Translator 2* (1), 45–63.

BMI et al. (Eds.). *Handbuch Dolmetschen im Asylverfahren*. Vienna: BMI/UNHCR/ÖVGD/ITAT.

Bot, H. (2005). *Dialogue interpreting in mental health*. Amsterdam: Rodopi.

Chesterman, A. (1993). From "is" to "ought": Laws, norms and strategies in translation studies. *Target 5* (1), 1–20.
Diriker, E. (2004). *De-/Re-contextualizing conference interpreting: Interpreters in the ivory tower?* Amsterdam: John Benjamins.
Fenton. S. (2004). Expressing a well-founded fear: Interpreting in convention refugee hearings. In G. Hansen, K. Malmkjær & D. Gile (Eds.), *Claims, changes and challenges in translation studies* (pp. 265–269). Amsterdam: John Benjamins.
Hale, S. (2004). *The discourse of court interpreting: Discourse practices of the law, the witness and the interpreter.* Amsterdam: John Benjamins.
Harris, B. (1990). Norms in interpretation. *Target 2* (1), 115–119.
Hertog, E. (Ed.). (2003). *Aequalitas. Equal access to justice across language and culture in the EU. Grotius project 2001/GRP/015.* Antwerp: Lessius Hogeschool.
Inghilleri, M. (2003). Habitus, field and discourse: Interpreting as a socially situated activity. *Target 15* (2), 243–268.
Inghilleri, M. (2005). Mediating zones of uncertainty: Interpreter agency, the interpreting habitus and political asylum adjudication. *The Translator 11* (1), 69–85.
Kälin, W. (1986). Troubled communication: Cross-cultural misunderstandings in the asylum-hearing. *International Migration Review 20* (2), 230–241.
Krainz, K., & Wintersberger, U. (2006). Das Asylverfahren in Österreich. In BMI et al. (Eds.), *Handbuch Dolmetschen im Asylverfahren* (pp. 20–28). Vienna: BMI/UNHCR/ÖVGD/ITAT.
Maryns. K. (2006). *The asylum speaker. Language in the Belgian asylum procedure.* Manchester, UK: St. Jerome.
Maurer-Kober, B. (2004). *Die aktuelle Praxis des Dolmetschens in Asylverfahren vor dem UBAS: Eine Bestandsaufnahme.* Unpublished master's thesis, University of Vienna.
Maurer-Kober, B. (2006). Rechtlicher Rahmen der Beiziehung von DolmetscherInnen im Asylverfahren. In BMI et al. (Eds.), *Handbuch Dolmetschen im Asylverfahren* (pp. 18–20). Vienna: BMI/UNHCR/ÖVGD/ITAT.
Metzger, M. (1999). *Sign language interpreting: Deconstructing the myth of neutrality.* Washington, DC: Gallaudet University Press.
Monnier, M.-A. (1995). The hidden part of asylum seekers' interviews in Geneva, Switzerland. *Journal of Refugee Studies 8* (3), 305–325.
Nord, C. (1997). *Translating as a purposeful activity: Functionalist approaches explained.* Manchester, UK: St. Jerome.
Pöllabauer, S. (2004). Interpreting in asylum hearings: Issues of role, responsibility and power. *Interpreting 6* (2), 143–180.
Pöllabauer, S. (2005). *"I don't understand your English, Miss." Dolmetschen bei Asylanhörungen.* Tübingen: Gunter Narr.

Reischl, K. (2001). *Kommunikationsbedingungen im Asylverfahren.* Published doctoral dissertation, University of Bielefeld, Berlin.
Roy, C. B. (2000). *Interpreting as a discourse process.* Oxford: Oxford University Press.
Scheffer, T. (2001). *Asylgewährung. Eine ethnographische Verfahrensanalyse.* Stuttgart: Lucius & Lucius.
UNHCR. (1995). *Interviewing applicants for refugree status (RLD 4).* Retrieved December 30, 2006 from http://www.unhcr.org/publ/PUBL/3ae6bd670.pdf.
Wadensjö, C. (1998). *Interpreting as interaction.* London: Longman.

Appendix

Excerpts from the corpus are identified by a four-character key for the hearing and by the start and finish times, in minutes and seconds, in the audio file. Participants are referred to with the following abbreviations:

ADJ	=	adjudicating official
APP	=	appellant (i.e. asylum seeker)
INT	=	interpreter
REC	=	recording clerk

Our translations of German utterances appear in *italics.*

Transcription conventions were applied as follows:

underlining	overlapping speech (e.g.: APP word word word INT word word word)
(→INT)	addressee of (part of) utterance
ə	voiced hesitation ("uh")
. .	short pause (. . = approx. 1 sec.)
°°	pausing for recording clerk (°° = approx. 1 sec.)
wo-, word-	false start or interruption
(?word)	uncertain
(? ?)	unrecoverable speech

Court Interpreting and Face: An Analysis of a Court Interpreter's Strategies for Conveying Threats to Own Face

Bente Jacobsen

The study presented in this article is part of an empirical study (Jacobsen, forthcoming) of face in an interpreter-mediated speech event in an adversarial courtroom: a prosecutor's questioning of a defendant in a criminal trial in a Danish district court.[1] One of the characteristics of the adversarial courtroom is the power differential between the lawyers in the courtroom, judges, prosecutors, and defense counsel, and the non-lawyers, defendants and witness. The Danish courtroom is less adversarial than many other courtrooms around the world, as the law puts certain constraints on lawyers' questioning strategies.[2] However, as in many other legal systems, cases are based on oral evidence that is presented mainly in the form of questions and answers. Thus, evidence extracted by lawyers questioning defendants and witnesses play a significant part in the outcome of a case. Furthermore, the law dictates a role-play and a questioning procedure that enables the questioners, the lawyers, to control the speech exchange to a high degree.

Danish law grants defendants in criminal trials certain rights and privileges. Thus, whereas witnesses are obliged to answer all questions put to them and face punishment if they perjure themselves,[3] defendants are not obliged to answer questions and cannot be punished for giving

1. Danish district courts are courts of first instance and hear both civil and criminal cases. A district court usually sits with three judges, one presiding (judicial) judge and two lay judges.

2. The Danish Administration of Justice Act, sections 184 and 752.

3. The Danish Administration of Justice Act, section 181, and the Danish Criminal Code, section 158.

false evidence.[4] Moreover, lawyers are not allowed to ask questions of defendants in a manner that implies that their refusal to answer questions or to acknowledge particular facts may be considered an admission of guilt.[5] However, despite these constraints, there is a clear power differential between the lawyers, whose designated role is to ask questions, and who represent the legal system and are present in their legal capacity, and the non-lawyers, whose designated role is to answer questions. Non-lawyers have been summoned to appear (though they may of course have come forward voluntarily) and who are outsiders to the legal system and generally unfamiliar with the specifics of the law (unless a defendant or a witness is a lawyer or a police officer, or a witness appears as an expert witness). Consequently, given the specified role of participants and the purpose of the event, i.e., the extraction of evidence, the questioning of defendants and witnesses provide multiple challenges to face, within the framework of Brown and Levinson's (1987) politeness theory.

THE CONCEPT OF FACE

According to Brown and Levinson (1987), all competent adults have and know each other to have face, that is, "the public self-image" that everyone wishes to claim for himself. Essentially, face consists of two main related aspects: negative face, which is the basic claim "to freedom of action and freedom from imposition," and positive face, which is "the positive consistent self-image or 'personality' (crucially including the desire that this self-image be appreciated and approved of) claimed by interactants" (Brown & Levinson, 1987, p. 61). Face is emotionally invested and may be lost, maintained, or enhanced, and must be constantly attended to in interaction (p. 61). Moreover, because of the mutual vulnerability of face (everyone's face depends on everyone else's being maintained), interactants generally engage in face-work, that is, communication strategies that will protect, maintain or enhance face, or mitigate face-threats (p. 61). Finally, because some speech acts are inherently face-threatening, e.g., orders that inherently threaten the receiver's face

4. The Danish Administration of Justice Act, sections 752 and 754, and the Danish Criminal Code, section 159(1).

5. The Danish Administration of Justice Act, section 752 (3).

or admission of guilt which inherently threaten the speaker's own face, interactants may engage in redressive action, that is, communication strategies intended to redress potential threats to positive or negative face (p. 101ff).

However, the degree of face threat is determined by the circumstances in which the threat occurs, rather than by the act itself, and Brown and Levinson (1987, p.74) identify three variables: (1) the degree of relationship, which is the social distance between speaker and receiver; (2) the power differential that details the position the speaker has over the receiver; and (3) the receiver's perception of the degree of threat,that is, the absolute amount of imposition of the act. .

Brown and Levinson's (1987) politeness theory has provided valuable insight, but has also met with some criticism, especially due to their (pp. 242–255) claim of universality, i.e., that their notion of face may be applied to all cultures. This claim has been contested by studies of politeness in non-Western societies which argue that Brown and Levinson's notion of negative politeness derives directly from the high value that Western cultures place on individual freedom and autonomy (e.g., Gu, 1990, p. 242; Kasper, 1990, p. 195). In addition, based on studies of politeness in Japanese and Chinese societies, Spencer-Oatey (2000, p. 14) argued that Brown and Levinson's notion of positive face needs to include a social identity element. Thus, Spencer-Oatey (pp. 13–14) argues that "face is associated with social/personal value" and consists of two interrelated aspects: (1) a desire for positive evaluation in terms of personal qualities such as competence, abilities, etc. (quality face), and (2) a desire for positive evaluation in terms of social identity or roles, such as standing within a group (identity face).

The different cultural conceptions of face are certainly important in multicultural exchanges. In the study presented in this article the defendant's mother tongue was Chinese, but he had requested an English interpreter and insisted upon speaking English throughout the trial, arguing that he was fluent in that language also, having lived most of his life in Great Britain. Consequently, it was necessary to consider whether Brown and Levinson's (1987) notion of face, if essentially Western, could apply to this defendant. However, though bearing in mind that at least some of the defendant's utterances might have been influenced by a Chinese notion of face rather than the notion of face relied on by Brown and Levinson (1987), this notion was nevertheless considered applicable because in terms of Spencer-Oatey's (2000) definition of face there was no evidence in the data to suggest that the defendant was particularly preoccupied with identity face. And the notion of quality face fits well with Brown and Levinson's (1987) notion of positive face. Moreover, the purpose of the questioning and the defendant's situation inevitably constrained his freedom of action. Finally, since the defendant had lived most of his life in Great Britain, he was presumably sensitive to Western face concerns.

Face in the Courtroom

The questioning of defendants presents an inherent threat to face in multiple ways. First, their negative face may be threatened by questions that request information that they are unable or unwilling to give. Second, their positive face may be threatened by questions that are designed to challenge their positive self-image as cooperative and trustworthy. Third, their negative face and positive face may be simultaneously threatened, for example by questions that suggest that their inability to provide required information constitutes attempts to mislead the court. Fourth, an attempt to protect positive face may put negative face at risk, and vice versa. Moreover, defendants' strategies to counter face-threats may result in the lawyer's face being threatened, and in turn, as the lawyer attempts to counter such threats, in a series of attacks and counterattacks that threaten the defendant.

Witnesses' face is similarly threatened (e.g., Mason & Stewart, 2001, pp. 56–64). Thus, the different status of defendants and witnesses and the fact that defendants generally have more at stake do not necessarily render one participant more vulnerable than the other as regards threats to face.

The lawyers in the courtroom also have to attend to face. They have to counter face-threats from defendants and witnesses and they have to attend to their own face as professionals. Their face is inherently threatened by any action that potentially jeopardizes their professional status.

THE COURT INTERPRETER AND FACE

A lawyer's questioning of a defendant or a witness with the assistance of a court interpreter constitutes a triadic speech event. Such events share certain contextual constraints, including the immediacy of the encounter, the physical presence of all three participants and the often sensitive nature of the topics discussed that are bound to exert considerable influence on the way meanings are exchanged and negotiated (e.g., Jacobsen, 2002). Not surprisingly, therefore, various studies of court interpreting (e.g., Berk-Seligson, 2002; Hale, 1997; Jacobsen, 2002; Morris, 1989) have shown that the common perception of the interpreter as a non-person, a kind of translating machine, often clashes with the reality of the interpreting situation in the courtroom. In addition, Wadensjö's (e.g., 1998) analysis of footing, applying Goffman's (1981) participation framework to interpreting in police interviews and medical interviews has provided major insight into the interpreter's role as translator and coordinator of the talk of others. Finally, these and other studies of triadic speech events have pointed to the significance of face and have suggested that interpreters are aware of the need for attending to their own face as well as the face of others. For example, Berk-Seligson's (2002, p. 140) study of English-Spanish exchanges in courtrooms in the United States shows how some court interpreters inserted polite forms when the receiver of their target texts was a judge, presumably feeling a need themselves for being polite when addressing judges. Moreover, Wadensjö (1998, pp. 177–179) demonstrates three different respects in which face-work came into play in a medical interview: (1) A primary participant displayed a wish to save face, and the interpreter had to convey this wish while interpreting; (2) the interpreter also had to attend to her own face as a professional (cf. lawyers' attention to face) to avoid jeopardizing the primary participants' confidence in her as a translator and coordinator; and (3) the interpreter's social identity, in addition to her role as interpreter, required her to save own face as well as the face of a primary participant (when questions about possible symptoms of a sexual disease caused embarrassment to her as well as to the patient).

This article contends, therefore, that, in certain situations, interpreters will attempt to clarify ambiguous utterances as well as mitigate threatening ones, and that they will do so not only to attend to the face of primary participants, but because they fear that the content of the utterances will reflect on them. They are motivated by the fear that ambiguous or confrontational utterances may be perceived by intended receivers as reflecting the professional skills or attitude of the interpreters, rather than the skills or attitude of the original speakers. Consequently, the aim of the study in this article has been to examine the court interpreter's strategies for conveying threats to her own face.

The Data

This author collected the data in November 1999, at Copenhagen City Court. The questioning was initially recorded on mini disc and then transcribed for the purpose of analysis. The languages involved were Danish and English. The court interpreter was an authorized interpreter,[6] i.e., a fully qualified and competent professional with some years of experience.

Three defendants appeared in the trial. All had Chinese as their mother tongue, but, as explained earlier the defendant in this study, hereafter referred to as *the defendant,* was assisted by an English interpreter. The other two defendants, hereafter referred to as *codefendant1* and *codefendant2,* were assisted by a Chinese interpreter.

The alleged offense was fraud. The three defendants allegedly used nine false credit cards to obtain a number of items from various shops in Copenhagen, and allegedly traveled to Denmark from Great Britain for this specific purpose. At the preliminary statutory hearing immediately following the defendants' arrest, the defendant and codefendant1 pleaded guilty as charged, whereas codefendant2 pleaded not guilty. His claim that he had never used any of the credit cards had been supported by his codefendants who also refused to say what he was doing in Copenhagen. Furthermore, each defendant denied any specific knowledge about the actions of the other two. Finally, the defendants refused to say who sent them to Denmark and/or who provided them with the plane tickets and the credit cards. The prosecutor believed that codefendant2 might have been that person, however, or at the very least that he had been in Copenhagen to supervise the actions of the other two, and thus he played a much more active role than either defendant was prepared to admit.

THE ANALYSIS

Not surprisingly, a great number of the prosecutor's questions potentially or directly threatened the defendant's negative and/or positive face, requiring him to react by opting out or by engaging in face-protecting strategies. In addition, the defendant's face-protecting strategies often

6. The official title is *state-authorized translator and interpreter.*

resulted in threats to the prosecutor's face, also requiring her to react. Finally, some of the face-protecting strategies of these two primary participants resulted in potential threats to the interpreter's face, which may have influenced her strategies for conveying the face-work of these participants. Extracts 1 to 8 present and discuss some these strategies.

The first two extracts demonstrate how, as the result of the defendant's request for clarification of the prosecutor's intention, the interpreter takes it upon herself to clarify, possibly in an attempt to save her own face as well as the face of the original speaker, the prosecutor. The question in Extract 1 relates to the defendant's status of employment. Since he was unemployed, which carries negative implications in Western societies including Britain and Denmark, this question potentially threatened his positive face. His resulting face-protecting strategies simultaneously threatened the prosecutor's and the interpreter's face:

Extract 1[7]

P: and what do you do?
og hvad laver du egentlig?
I: what is your job, your profession?
D: er my last profession or whatever?
I: in general.
D: I I was a company director. my company was registered in the company house in <country>.
I: yes.
ja.
D: and they trade restaurants.
I: yes. I mean I was er manager of a er company which did busi- er ran restaurants in in <country>, and it is a registered company hous-
ja. altså jeg har været øh direktør for et øh selskab der drev virk- øh drev restauranter i i <country>, og det er et registreret firma hus-

The defendant's initial reaction to the prosecutor's question was to ask for clarification, which may have been a stalling tactic, intended to protect his face: On the one hand, neither the original question nor the translation specified a point in time, which left room for multiple interpretations,

7. P = prosecutor, D = defendant, I = interpreter. See Appendix 1 for transcription symbols.

for example "what do you do right now," or "what do you generally do." On the other hand, when the interpreter took it upon herself to clarify,[8] relaying the question as a request for general information, which to some extent mitigated the potential threat, he responded by providing specific information about his last profession. Moreover, he provided a long and detailed answer and was seemingly so intent on getting his point across that he ignored the prosecutor's second question, thus threatening her negative face by resisting her attempt at taking the turn.

By requesting clarification, the defendant potentially threatened the positive face of both the prosecutor and the interpreter, by jeopardizing their role as competent professionals because his request potentially implicated that the original question was ambiguous or that it was mistranslated. As stated, his request was never translated to the prosecutor, though she was presumably aware of it. She may have been attempting to clarify the prosecutor's intention and/or re-establish her own role as a translator and coordinator. Consequently, the defendant's request for clarification may have been a face-protecting strategy, which by threatening the face of the prosecutor and/or the interpreter, resulted in the interpreter adopting a face-protecting strategy, which by mitigating the original question, ultimately offered some protection to the defendant's face.

Similarly in Extract 2:

Extract 2

P: why did you have to er book both rooms for- for all of you?
hvorfor skulle du øh booke begge værelser for- for jer alle sammen?
I: why did you have to er book both rooms for all of you?
D: sorry?
I: why did you have to book both rooms for all? all of you?
D: no comments. I just do.
I: erm, I have no comments to that. I just did.
øhm, det har jeg ikke kommentarer til. det gjorde jeg bare.

8. The prosecutor allowed the interpreter's clarification, possibly because she understood what was going on and/or the interpreter relayed her intention. The clarification nevertheless constitutes a violation of interpreter ethics (Jacobsen, 2002, p. 61). Danish courts tend to allow this kind of dialogue, however, especially when the foreign language is English, a language with which many lawyers and judges are familiar, and when the interpreter is a competent professional (Jacobsen, 2002, pp. 97–98).

The prosecutor's question relates to the fact that, following the three defendants' arrival in Denmark, the defendant checked all of them into a particular hotel. Once more, the defendant's request for clarification may have been an attempt at stalling, and again the interpreter took it upon herself to comply with his request, possibly once again motivated by a need to attend to her own positive face as well as the positive face of the prosecutor. However, when she repeated the question, she increased the force of the original, emphasizing *all of you?*. The defendant responded by opting out, thus threatening his own positive face. When the interpreter mitigated his opting out by completing his fragmented first utterance, she may again have been motivated by a need for saving face. She might have been concerned that the positive face of the defendant and her own positive face in the event that the defendant's opting out would be perceived as a reflection of her lack of proper interpreting skills.

Extracts 3 and 4 demonstrate how the prosecutor's requests for confirmation of some of the content of the defendant's answer were omitted by the interpreter in what might have been an attempt to save her own positive face as well as the face of the intended receiver, the defendant.

Extract 3

P: about a year? yes? and what about <codefendant1>, how- how long have you have you er known him?
cirka et år? ja? og hvad med <codefendant1>, hvor- hvor lang tid har du har du øh kendt ham?

I: and what about <codefendant1>, for how long time have you known him?

D: I know him on <date>.

I: er I met him <date>.
øh jeg mødte ham <date>.

The prosecutor's three utterances in Extract 3 immediately follow a statement from the defendant that he had known codefendant2 for about a year.[9] By twice requesting confirmation of some of the content of the defendant's previous answer *about a year? yes?* (*cirka et år? ja?*), the

9. For the purpose of this analysis, an utterance is defined as a stretch of speech preceded and followed by a terminating or a questioning intonation (cf. Appendix 1).

prosecutor managed to implicate that this answer was odd, suggesting, in turn, that it might be untrue. Thus, her requests directly threatened his positive face. However, the prosecutor's requests, and thus the implication they carried, were not conveyed to the defendant by the interpreter, whose rendition incidentally contained a grammatical error: *for how long time*. Presumably, grammatical errors of this kind are not uncommon in interpreting situations (or in other kinds of spoken interaction) that require fast, almost instantaneous production and understanding. In any case, in all probability, the interpreter perceived the requests, as they were audible on the mini disc. They did not carry particular emphasis compared to the subsequent utterance, however, and she may thus have failed to realize their significance and, focusing on what she perceived as the prosecutor's intention, such as a request for information about codefendant1, she consciously or unconsciously omitted what she may have considered to be redundant information. On the other hand, she may very well have realized their significance, and her omission may thus have been motivated by a wish for not appearing confrontational, fearing perhaps that the content of the requests would be perceived as reflecting her attitude rather than the prosecutor's.

Similarly in Extract 4:

Extract 4

P: ¤but presumably you met at the airport?¤
¤men I mødtes vel ude i lufthavnen?¤
I: but you met in the airport. *is that correct?*
D: yes?
I: yes.
ja.
P: *you did.* and you- you knew when you were leaving for for Denmark that<codefendant1> also had some credit cards on him?
**det gjorde du.* og I- du vidste godt da I skulle af sted til til Danmark at <codefendant1> også havde nogen kreditkort på sig?*
I: and you also knew it, when you left for Denmark, that <codefendant1> also had some credit cards in his possession. is that correct?
D: er, (. .) #I don't know what he has got, in his pocket.#
I: I mean I don't know what he has got in his pockets.
#altså jeg ved ikke hvad han har i sine lommer.#

According to Brown and Levinson (1987, p. 164), the prosecutor's inclusion in her first question of what they refer to as a Quality hedge, that is, addressed to Grice's (1975) maxim of Quality ('Try to make your contribution one that is true'), *presumably* (*vel*), not only suggests that she was not taking responsibility for the truth of the content of that question, but also asked whether a cooperative condition had in fact been met: The defendant had acknowledged that they all three flew to Denmark together, on the same plane, so by suggesting the possibility that all three defendants met at the airport, the prosecutor also suggested that the credit cards and the plane tickets were handed out there, and in turn that all three defendants were present when it happened, as well as the person or persons who handed them out. In addition, the connective *but* (*men*), marking contrast (Schiffrin, 1988, p. 152ff), implicated a contradiction between the defendant's negation and her suggestion. As a result, the prosecutor managed to imply that the defendant was being less than truthful, and in turn, that he was deliberately attempting to mislead the court, an implication that was strengthened by her tone of voice which conveyed surprise, or even incredulity.

The full implication of the question was not conveyed to the defendant, however, due to the interpreter's omission of the Quality hedge (cf. Brown & Levinson, 1987, p. 164) and her neutral tone of voice. Instead she added the tag question *is that correct?,* which indicated that ratification of the information in her first utterance was required. Thus, Hale (2004, p. 45) explains that tag questions are a type of yes-no questions that "express maximum conduciveness," since they are formed by a statement and an appended question with either a negative or a positive orientation. Citing Quirk et al. (1985, p. 814) and Hale (2004, pp. 46–48) further explains that the added tag constitutes an invariant tag question, a type of question that is used to seek confirmation of the statement and that usually contains no "contentious information." However, the tag question in Extract 4 indicated that the defendant was required to confirm information that was potentially controversial and could lead to other, more damaging information. Consequently, it may have served to suggest, like the Quality hedge, that the interpreter did not take responsibility for the truth content of the statement in her first utterance, which may explain why the defendant responded with the affirmative *yes,* with a questioning intonation, and thus answered a question with a question. This strategy implied that the prosecutor's question was surprising, or possibly irrelevant, threatening her positive face. On the other hand, the fact that the tag was spoken in a low voice may have indicated to the defendant that, rather than question his cooperative intention, the interpreter was expressing doubt about the correctness of her translation, or doubt about the correctness of the content of the original question, rather than doubt about his cooperative intention. Of course, if her addition was in fact meant to express doubt about the correctness of her translation, she may have been attending to own positive face, attempting to establish herself as a competent professional, willing to take responsibility for translation errors and, in turn, correct such errors. Since she did not explicitly express this intention; however, if it were indeed her intention, the defendant would presumably have attributed the content of her utterance to the original speaker, the prosecutor, anyway. Finally, quite possibly the interpreter was merely intending to protect the defendant's face, as well as her own face (not wanting to appear confrontational), by mitigating the threat in the original utterance.

In any case, the defendant's affirmative response, spoken with a questioning intonation, was conveyed with a terminating intonation, which eliminated the original implication and threat to the prosecutor's face, and again the interpreter may have been motivated by a need for not appearing confrontational. The prosecutor now proceeded with another attack, and her first utterance *you did?* (*det gjorde du?*), though spoken in a low voice, again threatened the defendant's positive face by repeating the information in his affirmative response, thus emphasizing this information, and in turn, the previous implication that he was deliberately attempting to mislead the court. Her second utterance, which suggested the possibility that he knew about his codefendant's credit cards, which in turn, implicated that the credit cards were handed out in the manner described above, threatened both his negative and positive face. The interpreter omitted the prosecutor's first utterance, however, but again added a tag question *is that correct?* Again, the tag indicated that the defendant was required to confirm information which was potentially controversial and could lead to other, more damaging information, so once more it may have suggested that the interpreter did not take responsibility for the truth content of the statement in her first utterance. Moreover, this addition was not spoken in a low voice, and was thus less likely to have been perceived as expressing doubt about the correctness of the translation, as well as less likely to mitigate the original threat, if this was the intention. In any case, the defendant must have perceived that his face was threatened because he took steps to protect it, implying after some hesitation (4 seconds) that the question was unreasonable, which presented a threat to the prosecutor's positive face. The force of his statement was strengthened by his tone of voice, which clearly registered annoyance. This time, the interpreter conveyed the defendant's intention, though her tone of voice registered a lesser degree of annoyance. First, she omitted the defendant's initial hesitation, the voice-filled pause, and the pause. Second, she included the filler *I mean* (*altså*). Schiffrin (1988, p. 295ff) explains that this filler potentially indicates a certain attitude on the part of the speaker towards the interaction, part of the interaction, or the addressee, or addressees, since it marks a speaker's modification of his ideas and intentions and is used to maintain speaker and hearer focus on this information. Consequently, the filler added a degree of hesitancy that potentially strengthened the implication of annoyance.

The next Extracts, 5 and 6, demonstrate how the defendant's ambiguous utterances, intended to protect his face, are modified by the interpreter, again possibly in an attempt to save her own positive face as well as his face:

Extract 5

P: you say you come here by plane, how who bought the plane ticket?
du siger I kommer hertil med fly, hvordan hvem købte flybilletten?

I: so you- you said you came by plane, who bought the plane ticket for you?

D: I was given the ticket e:r, together with the credit cards.

I: I mean well, someone gave me the plane ticket together with the credi- credit cards.
altså ja, der var en der gav mig flybilletten sammen med kredi- kreditkortene.

The prosecutor's question threatens the defendant's negative and positive face by requesting information about the mastermind behind the fraud. The defendant was faced with a dilemma: opt out and be perceived as uncooperative, or answer without revealing the identity of the mastermind. As it happened, his face-protecting strategy was to answer in the passive, thus omitting to indicate an agent. For some reason, the interpreter chose to convey his answer in the active, though, indicating an agent: *someone* (*en*). Furthermore, she added *I mean well* (*altså ja*), which indicated a need for maintaining focus and a need for building coherence. Thus, Schiffrin (1998, p. 102ff) explains that *well* is a response marker that indicates a speaker's awareness of the need for building coherence, and for anchoring him into the interaction precisely at those points where upcoming coherence is not granted. In other words, possibly aware that the defendant's utterance might be perceived as an attempt at misleading the court, and fearing that this might reflect on her skills or attitude as a professional court interpreter, she mitigated a potential threat to his positive face as well as her own face.

The question in Extract 6 relates to the defendant's personal gain from the fraud scheme. Having established that the defendant was to get 10% of every item that he purchased with the false credit cards, the prosecutor asked him if he kept an account of his purchases. Since no account was included in the presented evidence, the implication of her question threatened both his negative and positive face. The logical conclusion to his statement would be that someone had to have kept an account. However, if he acknowledged that he or one of his codefendants had kept it, he would presumably have to explain its whereabouts. Furthermore, if he acknowledged that one of his codefendants had kept it, his acknowledgment might be taken as an admission that he and his codefendants presented false statements regarding their knowledge of each other's actions. On the other hand, if he denied having kept one, his denial might be taken to imply that one of his codefendants kept it, and thus the implication of his denial would be the same as before. In addition, his denial might also be perceived as an indirect admission that his statement about the 10% represented a lie.

The defendant finally provided the hesitant and incomplete answer in Extract 6, which clearly reflects his dilemma:

Extract 6

D: I (.), I I wrote, I mean, I I did not but I usually do. at the end of the:, when I finish all the:,

I: erm, I mean, I didn't do it but but I <u>normally do when I have finished shopping</u>.
øhm, altså (.), jeg gjorde det ikke men men det gør jeg <u>normalt når jeg er færdig med at købe ind</u>.

D: <u>I know approximately</u>. I know approximately.

I: er but I know approximately how much.
øh men jeg ved cirka hvor meget.

The defendant began by stating that he wrote something down, and then proceeded to deny that he had kept an account. Thus, he managed to avoid committing himself to any definite action. Moreover, the contradiction in his statement was emphasized by his *I mean,* indicating a need for maintaining focus (cf. Extract 4), and his *usually,* which implicated *normally.* The interpreter's course of action was to complete his fragmented utterance, presumably in an attempt to make his communicative intention available or more available to the prosecutor (cf. Jacobsen, 2002, p. 272) and deliver it slightly less hesitantly, thus potentially increasing the force of the original. Again, she may have been attending to her own positive face, fearing that a fragmented rendition would be perceived as the result of her lack of proper interpreting skills. In any case, she omitted the first two parts of his utterance, where he admitted to writing something down, and thus she failed to render what might have been an important piece of evidence: *I, I wrote.*

The defendant then proceeded to claim that there was no need for an account, twice stating *I know approximately,* presumably because of the overlap. Apparently, the interpreter again attempted to complete his utterance, possibly for the same reasons as before. Moreover, her inclusion of *but* (*men*) served to strengthen the defendant's claim by indicating a contrast between this and the denial in his previous statement (cf. Extract 4).

Finally, Extracts 7 and 8 demonstrate how the prosecutor's face-threatening questions are mitigated by the interpreter. The action in Extract 7 immediately follows the action in Extract 6. Interestingly, the interpreter's strategy here was to modify both the threatening question and the ensuing answer, decreasing not only the force of the question, but also the force of the defendant's face-protecting utterance:

Extract 7

P: okay, what do you mean by normally, have you done this before?
okay, hvad mener du med normalt, har du gjort det her før?

I: er what do you mean by normally, have you (.) done this before?

D: no, no, that was in my mind.

I: er no-
øh nej-

D: that I was going to do it. but because, you know, things get confused sometimes.

I: er, no. er but it was what I- what I had thought a little about doing. er but because everything became so confusing then: well. then I didn't have time to do it.
øh, nej. øh men det var hvad jeg- hvad jeg havde tænkt lidt at gøre. øh men fordi det hele blev så forvirret så: ja. så nåede jeg det ikke.

The prosecutor's question threatened the defendant's positive face, by implicating that he had committed a similar offense, or offenses, at some earlier time, which in turn, implicated that his earlier statement to the effect that this was his first offense represented a lie. The implication was further strengthened by her *okay,* which here functions as a frame, marking a boundary in the discourse and signaling a change of topic (Stenström, 1994, pp. 67, 85–86). However, the interpreter omitted *okay* and included a voice-filled pause and a pause, adding a degree of hesitancy, thus mitigating the threat, again possibly to protect her own positive face, as well as the face of the intended receiver, the defendant, who nevertheless perceived that his face was threatened, and took steps to protect it. Thus, his first two utterances implied that he had intended to keep an account, while his last utterance *but because, you know, things get confused sometimes* constituted a blatant flout of Grice's (1975) first maxim of Quantity ('Make your contribution as informative as is required') generating the implication that he did not have the opportunity to keep an account, and, in turn, that he did not keep one. The interpreter explicated this implication *then I didn't have time to do it* (*så nåede jeg det ikke*) and included the adverb *a little* (*lidt*), which deemphasized the implication that he had intended to keep an account. She also included three voice-filled pauses, and included *well* just before rendering the implication, indicating a need for building coherence. Consequently, her target text was more hesitant than the original and further indicated that the defendant was aware that he might not have provided the required answer. Thus, whether or not her additions here, like her additions in Extract 6 above, were motivated by a need for protecting her own positive face, as well as the face of the defendant, she presented a target text which served to increase the threat to the defendant's face by potentially indicating that he was being less than truthful.

In Extract 8, the prosecutor's questions relate to three suitcases purchased by the defendants for storing the purchased items. The prosecutor attempted to establish which defendant had been in possession of which suitcase, presumably attempting via this evidence to throw further light on the role of codefendant2. The defendant was not particularly forthcoming, and at one point the prosecutor asked:

Extract 8

P: were you hauling two suitcases?
har du slæbt rundt på to kufferter?
I: have you been er carrying around two suitcases?
D: at one stage I was carrying two suitcases.
I: I mean at-
altså på-
D: at one stage.
I: at one time I had two suitcases. erm on me or-
på et tidspunkt der havde jeg to kufferter. øhm på mig eller-
P: but could you also after the same- have met with er <codefendant1> or <codefendant2>, and then subsequently then have asked them to carry these roller skates and put them over in a different suitcase?
men kan du også efter den samme- har mødtes med øh <codefendant1> eller <codefendant2>, og så efterfølgende så har bedt dem om at bære de her rulleskøjter og lagt dem over i en anden kuffert?
I: but could it also be so that you met er <codefendant1> or <codefendant2>, and then you have asked one of them to take the roller blades and carry them for you.
D: maybe.
I: maybe.
måske.

The prosecutor's choice of words, *lugging* (*slæbt rundt på*), in her first question implicated that it would have meant great discomfort to carry two suitcases and therefore that it was unlikely that two of three suitcases had been his. However, perhaps again not wanting to appear confrontational, the interpreter translated her words into *carrying,* thus decreasing the force of the original. Consequently, the defendant responded by contradicting the prosecutor's implication, without acknowledging whether the two suitcases had in fact been his suitcases. His *at one stage* thus implicated 'not all the time,' and this implication was repeated in his second utterance, emphasizing it. However, the force of his utterance was decreased by the interpreter. First, though her initial *I mean* (*altså*) added hesitance and potentially indicated annoyance (cf. Extract 4), this may not have been perceived by the prosecutor, due to the overlap. Second, she omitted the defendant's second utterance, presumably due to the overlap. Third, she added a hesitant and fragmented utterance, which may have been an attempt to provide repair, and thus an attempt at protecting her own positive face, having translated *was carrying* into *had,* which did not necessarily imply "carry." In other words, her translation strategy, which potentially intended to protect her own positive face, decreased the force of the defendant's face-protecting strategy (cf. Extract 7). Therefore, the prosecutor persisted and provided yet another face-threatening utterance, again emphasized by *but* (*men*) (cf. Extract 4). However, she mitigated her threat by including *could you also* (*kan du også*) suggesting possibility, not certainty. Again, the interpreter decreased the force of the original, omitting *and put them in a different suitcase?* (*og lagt dem over i en anden kuffert?*). The defendant nevertheless took steps to protect his face once again, his *maybe* merely acknowledging possibility, not certainty.

Interestingly, this final extract demonstrated how the interpreter employed translation strategies which decreased the force of original utterances to a degree, where she not only potentially managed to protect her own positive face and the face of the primary participants, but also very much influenced the face-work of these participants.

CONCLUSION

This article presented an analysis of face in a triadic speech event in an adversarial courtroom. The adopted approach was to examine the court interpreter's strategies for conveying potential threats to their own face by focusing on those instances where the face-work of a primary participant resulted in threats to the interpreter's face as well as the face of the original speaker or the intended receiver. The results suggest that the interpreter's modifications of face-threatening and face-protecting utterances were frequently motivated by a need for saving her own face as well as the face of one of the primary participants. Thus, the results appear to support the contention presented in this article that court interpreters are attentive to their own face and, in certain situations, will attempt to clarify ambiguous utterances as well as mitigate threatening ones. They are motivated by fear that ambiguous or confrontational utterances may be perceived by intended receivers as reflecting the professional skills or attitude of the interpreters, rather than the skills or attitude of the original speakers.

Of course, the study in this article has its limitations, as the analysis is based on the recorded data and the author's own observations only. To strengthen the results, therefore, methodological triangulation is required. Further research will need to combine various methods of data collection such as questionnaires and/or follow-up interviews with court interpreters, asking them to explore conscious and unconscious influences of face. In addition, the hypothesis that court interpreters are conscious of face and attentive to own face as well as the face of primary participants may need to be tested by conducting a number of experimental studies. Finally, future studies will need to look at the consequences of court interpreters' modifications of face-threatening and face-protecting utterances to determine the influence of these modifications on, for example, the direction of the talk exchange, the credibility of primary speakers and/or perceptions of their competence, and the power differential between the lawyers and non-lawyers in the courtroom.

REFERENCES

Berk-Seligson, S. (2002). *The bilingual courtroom. Court interpreters in the judicial process.* Chicago: University of Chicago Press.

Brown, P., & Levinson, S. C. (1987). *Politeness. Some universals in language usage.* Cambridge: Cambridge University Press.

Goffman, E. (1981). *Forms of talk.* Oxford: Basil Blackwell.

Grice, H. P. (1975). Logic and conversation. In P. Cole & J. L. Morgan (Eds.), *Syntax and semantics 3: Speech acts* (pp. 41–58). New York: Academic Press.

Gu, Y. (1990). Politeness phenomena in modern Chinese. *Journal of Pragmatics 14*, 237–257.

Hale, S. (1997). The treatment of register variation in court interpreting. *The Translator 3* (1), 39–54.

Hale, S. (2004). *The discourse of court interpreting. Discourse practices of the law, the witness and the interpreter.* Amsterdam: John Benjamins.

Jacobsen, B. (2002). *Pragmatic meaning in court interpreting: An empirical study of additions in consecutively-interpreted question-answer dialogues.* Published doctoral dissertation, The Aarhus School of Business, Denmark.

Jacobsen, B. (2008). Interactional pragmatics and court interpreting: An analysis of face. Doing justice to court interpreting [Special issue]. *Interpreting 10* (1), 128–158.

Kasper, G. (1990). Linguistic politeness: Current research issues. *Journal of Pragmatics 14*, 193–218.

Mason, I., & Stewart, M. (2001). Interactional pragmatics, face and the dialogue interpreter. In I. Mason (Ed.), *Triadic exchanges. Studies in dialogue interpreting* (pp. 51–70). Manchester, UK: St. Jerome.

Morris, R. (1989). Court interpretation: The trial of Ivan John Demjanjuk. A case study. *The Interpreters' Newsletter 2*, 27–37.

Quirk, R., GreenBaum, S., Leech, G., & Svartvik, J. (1985). *A comprehensive grammar of the English language*. London: Longman.

Retsplejeloven [The Danish Administration of Justice Act]. (2006).

Schiffrin, D. (1988). *Discourse markers*. Cambridge: Cambridge University Press.

Spencer-Oatey, H. (2000). Rapport management: A framework for analysis. In H. Spencer-Oatey (Ed.), *Culturally speaking: Managing rapport through talk across cultures* (pp. 11–45). London: Continuum.

Stenström, A.-B. (1994). *An introduction to spoken interaction*. London: Longman.

Straffeloven (The Danish Criminal Code). (2006).

Wadensjö, C. (1998). *Interpreting as interaction*. London: Longman.

Appendix

Transcription Symbols

.	"Terminating intonation" (usually with a falling tone), indicating that the speaker is prepared to relinquish the turn, or, at least, that an information unit has been completed.
?	"Questioning intonation" (usually with a rising tone), indicating that the speaker wants a response from the addressee.
,	"Continuing intonation" (usually with a rising or sustained tone, with or without a short pause), indicating that the information unit has not been completed and/or that the speaker does not want to relinquish the turn.
¤¤	Frames an utterance, or part of an utterance, and indicates that the framed part is spoken in a tone of voice which indicates surprise.

##	Frames an utterance, or part of an utterance, and indicates that the framed part is spoken in a tone of voice which indicates annoyance.
**	Frames an utterance or part of an utterance and indicates that the framed part is spoken in a low voice.
-	Indicates a sudden cut-off of the current sound.
:	Indicates that the sound just before has been noticeably lengthened.
(.)	Indicates a pause of less than a second.
(. .)	Indicates a pause of a second or more.
underlining	Indicates simultaneous talk.
boldface	Indicates emphasis.
italics	Original utterances or renditions in Danish.

Guilty or Not Guilty?

An Investigation of Deaf Jurors' Access

to Court Proceedings Via Sign Language

Interpreting

Jemina Napier and David Spencer

> The participation in juries by representatives of the community is a fundamental element of the administration of justice, and thus serves the interests of the State. Jury service, like voting, is a right and obligation of citizenship [of Australia]. (New South Wales Law Reform Commission, 2004, p. 2)

The institution of trial by jury, although not without critics, has been regarded for centuries as a fundamental part of the administration of justice. Its features are credited with helping to secure the protection

This project was made possible with funding from the Macquarie University External Collaborative Grant Scheme, in collaboration with the NSW Law Reform Commission. The success of this project owes a great debt to the participation, information and support from the following people: Hon Justice Michael Adams, Karin Banna, Sue Blackwell, Karen Bontempo, Chris Callaghan, Patricia Cangelosi-Williams, Andy Carmichael, Tony Clews, Caroline Conlon, Diana Eades, Sandra Feijoo Negron, A/Prof Sandra Hale, Peter Hennessy, Celise Hill, Rebecca Ladd, Jieun Lee, Maree Madden, Carla Mathers, Judy Maynard, Hugh McMullen, Ruth Morris, Gary Muldoon, John Olsson, Wendy Pickup, Collette Ryan, Virginia Signorelli, Bruce Shaw, Helen Slatyer, Nina Spies, David Stedman, Sandra Sweeney, Professor Michael Tillbury, Fabio Tonelli, Maurice Varney, Stafford Wales, Hon Justice James Wood, and Todd Wright. In particular, we would like to acknowledge the work of our research assistant, Joe Sabolcec, who made a significant contribution to all aspects of the study.

of the community from the tyranny of absolutism and the self-interest of the powerful, while reflecting democratic ideals and representing current social values and attitudes . . . The jury is thus a group of "ordinary" people, disinterested in the outcome of the trial, and independent of powerful and influential social forces. (NSWLRC, 2004, p. 13)

In most English-speaking countries, including Australia and the United Kingdom, non-English speakers are not allowed to serve as jurors as they cannot access the language of the court. So what about deaf people? Some may be competent English users, but not able to access the language of the court due to not being able to hear it. But they could access all other written information in the form of evidence, testimonies, written confessions, and so forth.

Currently, deaf persons cannot serve as jurors in Australia or in most other countries in the world. Debates over whether deaf people should be permitted to serve as jurors have long featured in legal journals (Golbas, 1981; Silas, 1993). Current policy in the majority of countries states that deaf people are not capable of serving as jurors, due to their "incapacity" or disability, that is, their hearing loss.

The United States has led the way with respect to law reform on this issue, with many states now allowing deaf people to serve as jurors, and with provisions for interpreters for deaf jurors (Ellman, 1992; LSS, 2000). Deaf people cannot serve as jurors in British or Irish Criminal Courts due to legal issues with having a 13th person (i.e., an interpreter) in the jury room (Deaf Blawg, 2006; Enright, 1999); however, a deaf woman has served as a juror in a British Coroner's Court (Barber, 2005).

With the introduction of the New Zealand Sign Language (NZSL) Bill before parliament in 2005 to have NZSL recognized as an official language and for use in legal proceedings,[1] a deaf man residing in New Zealand was permitted to serve as a juror for the first time in a tax fraud case ("Deaf Man," 2005). In an interview with the New Zealand National Equal Opportunities Network, David McKee stated that he had been "quite excited about the jury duty because [he] knew [he]'d be breaking down barriers and opening doors for other Deaf people who

1. The third and final reading of the NZSL Bill was passed on April 6, 2006, and received royal assent on April 10, 2006. The NZSL Act is thus now enshrined in New Zealand Law and recognizes NZSL as New Zealand's third official language alongside English and Te Reo Maori.

in the future wanted to participate" (NEON, 2006). He also acknowledged that the judge might have been open to having him on the jury, and interpreters in the court and jury room, because of the NZSL Bill (Travaglia, 2005).

LAW REFORM IN NEW SOUTH WALES, AUSTRALIA

Given that the notion of deaf people serving as jurors is obviously on the law reform agenda in some countries, the consideration given in Australia to this issue is timely. Acting at the request of the state of New South Wales (NSW)—the most populous state in Australia—Attorney General, the NSW Law Reform Commission (NSWLRC) established a reference group in 2003 to investigate whether deaf and blind persons ought to be able to serve on juries in criminal courts. The terms of reference were

> To inquire into and to report on whether persons who are profoundly deaf or have a significant hearing or sight impairment should be able to serve as jurors in New South Wales and, if so, in what circumstances. In undertaking this review, the Commission should have regard to the Anti-Discrimination Act 1977 (NSW), the Disability Discrimination Act 1992 (Commonwealth), and the need to maintain confidence in the administration of justice in New South Wales. (NSWLRC, 2004, p. v)

The reference group was comprised of members of the Criminal Division of the Supreme Court of NSW and representatives of other organizations, such as the NSW Association of the Deaf, People With Disabilities, and the Human Rights and Equal Opportunities Commission. An initial discussion paper was published in 2004 (NSWLRC, 2004), including submissions from various stakeholders such as the Deaf Society of NSW and the NSW Association of the Deaf.

In reviewing law reform concerning deaf jurors in other countries, the NSWLRC noted in the discussion paper that

> One issue relating to jury service by deaf people is that the presence of a sign language interpreter in the deliberation room violates the rule excluding persons other than the jurors in that room. In *Eckstein v Kirby*, the US District Court ruled that it did, noting that secrecy must be preserved to guarantee a vigorous and can-

did discussion of the issues by the jurors. However, some courts have held that the rule excluding persons other than jurors from the jury room during deliberations does not apply to sign language interpreters based on a number of reasons. First, the rule is said to apply in reality only to officers of the court such as bailiffs, judges, or counsel, who because of their (perceived or actual) capacity to influence the jurors, might inhibit free discussion. This danger would not arise in the case of an interpreter who performs a purely mechanical function, much like a hearing aid, microphone, or typewriter. Absent any evidence of inappropriate behavior on the part of an interpreter, the jurors are unlikely to perceive him or her as having any influence on or capacity to pressure any of them. Also, the judge may give instructions to both the interpreter and the jury that participation by the former is improper. Secondly, jury secrecy would not be endangered since there are legal and ethical rules preventing interpreters from revealing confidences made during jury deliberations. Finally, practical experience has shown that none of the anticipated problems have arisen. In those jurisdictions where deaf people have been sworn, interpreters accompanied the jurors in the jury room, and there has never been a breach of confidentiality, nor problems with the interpreter breaching the oath of non-involvement, nor any problem with respect to the panel not being able effectively to deliberate because of the presence of the interpreter. A number of States have adopted legislation or court rules allowing an interpreter to accompany a deaf juror during deliberations. Some contain safeguards such as specifying that the interpreter will only act to communicate for and to the juror with the disability, or should refrain from personal interjection and uphold the secrecy of the proceeding.(NSWLRC, 2004, pp.62–63)

Thus early on, the presence of an interpreter as a 13th person in the jury room was not considered to necessarily be an issue. However, although it was accepted that signed language interpreters are regularly used in criminal courts in order to provide witnesses, complainants, and defendants with access to court proceedings, it was felt that jurors require a different level of access to information. Jurors do not just need access to the proceedings in a courtroom, they need to make informed decisions about the status of a person's guilt in committing a crime, and need to be able to participate in jury deliberations; as stated in an American case *People v. Guzman.*

> At a minimum, a juror must be able to understand all of the evidence presented, evaluate that evidence in a rational manner, communicate effectively with the other jurors during deliberations, and comprehend the applicable legal principles, as instructed by the court. (NSWLRC, 2004, p. 12)

Given this difference, concerns were raised in relation to the interpretation of evidence, interpretation of the submissions of counsel, interpretation of a judge's directions to the jury, and interpretation of jury room deliberations. Essentially, questions were mooted about whether deaf people can sufficiently comprehend legal proceedings when relying on a signed language interpreter, in order to get full access to the facts of a case, and thus make an informed decision about a person's guilt.

The notion of whether hearing people can sufficiently comprehend court proceedings in order to effectively carry out their role as jurors was acknowledged in the discussion paper.

> Any juror may perform below the standard expected, due to such factors as his or her individual attention span, boredom threshold, lack of interest in the matter being tried, the trial's length, and unpredictable external events. Any juror may bring his or her prejudices, such as racism or distrust of police or authority, to the jury room. In addition . . . although using the same evidence, different jurors will reach different conclusions, despite having the use of the same senses. Nearly all commentators agree that juries have great difficulty understanding and applying judicial instructions. (NSWLRC, 2004, p. 5)

As a consequence of further reference group discussions it was decided that empirical evidence was needed to assess two key issues:

1. The translatability of legal concepts from English into Australian Sign Language (Auslan).
2. The ability for deaf jurors to access court proceedings through signed language interpreters.

The notion of deaf juror access to jury deliberations would be considered separately, as it was felt that the essential issues to address initially were related to accuracy and comprehension. Thus a pilot study was commissioned by the NSWLRC in order to explore the linguistic and interpreting issues faced by potential deaf jurors in accessing court proceedings. The overall goal of the study was to give consideration to deaf persons' access to court proceedings in the role of juror rather than as a complainant, defendant, or witness and to present evidence to support the appointment of deaf jurors in NSW Criminal Courts.

LITERATURE REVIEW

Legal Interpreting

The majority of research and discussion on legal interpreting in the spoken language interpreting literature focuses on court interpreting, with a reasonably large body of literature that discusses courtroom interpreting practice, the role of the court interpreter, and ethical dilemmas faced by court interpreters (e.g., Angelelli, 2004; Carroll, 1995; Colin & Morris, 1996; Edwards, 1995; Fenton, 1997; Fowler, 1997; Gonzalez, Vasquez, & Mikkelson, 1992; Kadric, 2000; Kelly, 2000; Lane, McKenzie-Bridle, & Curtis, 1999; Mathers, 2006; Mikkelson, 1998, 2000; Morris, 1999; Robinson, 1994; Schweda Nicholson, 1994).

There has been some discussion of other aspects of legal interpreting, such as solicitor-client interviews, police interviews, police interrogations and confessions, tribunals or immigration/ refugee hearings (Barsky, 1996; Fowler, 2003; Gibbons, 1995; Krouglov, 1999; Maley, Candlin, Koster, & Crichton, 1995; Pöllabauer, 2004; Shuy, 1998; Zambrano, 2006).

In Australia, there have been several publications which explore the cultural barriers for Aboriginal people in accessing court proceedings (Cooke, 2002; Eades, 2003; Fryer-Smith, 2002; Goldflam, 1995; Howard, Quinn, Blokland, & Flynn, 1993). In all aspects of legal interpreting, the person typically requiring the interpreter is the victim, witness, defendant or complainant; although there are cases of deaf lawyers relying on signed language interpreters (Kurlander, 2008).

With respect to deaf people's involvement in the legal system, there have been a number of publications that specifically discuss deaf people's access to justice via signed language interpreters (Banna, 2004; Brennan, 1999; Fournier, 1997; Miller, 2001; Miller & McCay, 1994; Nardi, 2005; Russell, 2002; Stevens, 2005; Tilbury, 2005; Turner, 1995; Turner & Brown, 2001; Wilcox, 1995); and Miller and McCay have contributed significantly with their discussions of the potential linguistic barriers that deaf people face in the legal system (McCay & Miller, 2001, 2005; Miller, 2003; Miller & McCay, 2001).

All of these discussions have focused on the deaf person as a member of a minority group being disadvantaged in accessing the legal system. In all of these publications, the role of the interpreter has been considered in light of the position of the client as a participant in the legal system as a defendant, witness, or complainant. None have considered what the role of an interpreter might be in working with a juror. This is more than likely due to the fact that non-English speaking people have not historically been allowed to serve on juries. This situation is beginning to change, and the notion of interpreting for jurors is discussed further in this chapter. Regardless of the role of the client, legal discourse will always provide challenges for interpreters of any language.

Legal Discourse

Legal discourse encompasses various relationships between language use and the realm of law. Forensic linguistics is the branch of linguistics that applies discourse analysis to legal contexts, and identifies clear features of linguistic behavior (Gibbons, 1999, 2003; Olsson, 2004; Shuy, 2001, 2003). The challenge for interpreters is not only related to legal terminology, but also to how language is used in legal contexts. Essentially, legal discourse consists of contextualized utterances that serve a certain primary communicative purpose. Legal language (or "legalese") differs from colloquial language on lexical, semantic, and syntactic levels, and in particular, the nature of courtroom interaction influences the type of language used.

The legal discourse used by lawyers and judges in the courtroom is often found to be too complicated for the layperson to comprehend. Berk-Seligson (1990) identifies a number of factors that lead to this level of complexity including the practice of oral legalese often being written to be read aloud. Danet (1980a), cited in Berk-Seligson, refers to nine lexical features of legal English: (1) technical terms; (2) common terms with an uncommon meaning; (3) words whose origin is Latin, French, or Old English; (4) polysyllabic words; (5) unusual prepositional phrases; (6) doublets (combination of Anglo-Saxon words with French or Latin words); (7) formality; (8) vagueness; and (9) over-precision.

Berk-Seligson (1990) also refers to 11 syntactic features of legal English: (1) nominalizations, (2) passive constructions; (3) conditionals; (4) unusual anaphora; (5) whiz deletion (deletion of relative pronouns); (6) high frequency of prepositional phrases and their unusual placement between the subject and predicate of a sentence; (7) lengthy sentences; (8) unique determiners; (9) impersonality; (10) wide variety of semantically negative words; and (11) parallel structure in the linking of words and phrases by means of conjunctions "or" and "and." Berk-Seligson also states that discourse features in legalese that contribute to incomprehensibility include lack of cohesion and overly compact sentences.

Further key features of legal discourse include: Information seeking, clarification, reframing, reformulation, paraphrasing, summarizing, option-presenting, questioning strategies, testimony as narrative, double negatives, hedges, hesitation fillers, polite forms, question-intonation statements, intensifiers, direct speech, and answering questions (is it not true that . . .), abrupt topic shifts and returns, use of tag questions, and use of silence (Conley & O'Barr, 1998; Drew, 1990; J. Gibbons, 2003; Tiersma, 1999).

The complexities of legal discourse present two challenges of interest to this study in relation to the key research questions:

- How well do lay people understand legal discourse?
- How accurately can interpreters convey the terminology, strategies, and conventions used in courtroom discourse in order to match the intention of the speaker?

Interpreting Courtroom Discourse

Several in-depth linguistic studies, with spoken and signed language interpreters, have explored the complexities involved when interpreting in court; with the analysis of pragmatics and discourse in courtrooms, and in particular the challenges of interpreting legalese.

Observation and analysis of English-Spanish interpreted interactions in the courtroom in the United States (Berk-Seligson, 1990, 2002) and in Australia (Hale, 1996, 1997a, 1997b, 1997c, 1999, 2001, 2002; Hale & Gibbons, 1999) have demonstrated that interpreters make a range of linguistic decisions during the interpreting process based on their understanding of courtroom discourse, which influences elements of the interaction, such as: turn taking, pragmatic force, interruptions or clarifications, variation in register, discourse markers, and politeness. Thus, as an inherent part of the process of interpreting, the interpreter alters the dynamics and therefore impacts on the interaction.

It has also been suggested that in influencing language and interaction in the courtroom, the interpreter challenges the authority of the court and the lawyers in the courtroom (Berk-Seligson, 1990; Brennan & Brown, 1997; Gibbons, 1999, 2003; Hale & Gibbons, 1999; Hale, 2004).

Brennan and Brown (1997) conducted a major study to assess the extent of deaf people's access to justice in the U.K. They observed British Sign Language (BSL) interpreters working in court, administered a survey of legal interpreters, and interviewed deaf people and interpreters about their legal interpreting experiences in police, court, and other legal settings. They highlighted the fact that signed language interpreters experience conflict in terms of perceptions of their role; but the most interesting aspect of their study is their discussion of linguistic issues. In addition to the linguistic and discourse challenges faced by interpreters of all languages, signed language interpreters work bimodally between two languages that are expressed in different modalities (i.e., spoken and visual-gestural). This presents further challenges for interpreters as they need to visually encode information into sign language that may be critical to a case, for example, did the murderer walk on the left or right hand side of the victim?

Brennan and Brown also observed the use of borrowing (also discussed by Brennan, 2001, in a separate paper), whereby interpreters utilize fingerspelling and lip patterns (mouthing) to borrow English words into BSL. These strategies have also been observed in deaf people and interpreters using American Sign Language (ASL) (Davis, 1990, 2003; Lucas & Valli, 1992), Italian Sign Language (LIS) (Fontana, 1999), and Auslan (Johnston, 2002; Napier, 2006). This borrowing strategy used by interpreters is what can be referred to as a *literal translation style*. This style is commonly used in contexts where participants need to access formal registers of language, technical terms, or context specific language use, such as university lectures (Napier, 2002).

Another significant investigation of signed language interpreting in court was conducted by Russell (2002). She investigated the accuracy of Canadian English-ASL interpretations in courtroom discourse by contrasting the outcomes of simultaneous and consecutive interpreting approaches.

In her study, Russell (2002) conducted four mock trials with real judges and lawyers, some with experience of working with spoken and signed language interpreters; and interpreters worked in either the consecutive or simultaneous mode. Three different discourse events were analyzed: (1) entering of direct evidence, (2) cross-examination, and (3) expert witness testimony. Russell found a statistically significant difference in terms of accuracy, with simultaneous interpretations 87% accurate, as compared with consecutive interpretations that were 95% accurate.

Post-trial interviews with participants revealed that the lawyers and judges seemed to prefer experiencing interpretation in the simultaneous mode, especially during the cross-examination (for the lawyers). They stressed the importance of preparation with interpreters, and that interpreters should request permission from the judge to clarify information, or consult with one another. Deaf witnesses said that interpreters should be confident and well prepared; whereas the expert witness felt that it was important to prepare with interpreters, and commented that they did not seem comfortable using the consecutive approach or notetaking. The interpreters also stressed the importance of preparation, and recognized that the quality of their interpreting was better when they used the consecutive mode.

In summary, Russell stated that interpreters should recognize the value of using consecutive or simultaneous interpreting techniques for different discourse types in court, and should negotiate carefully with lawyers and judges about what strategies to use and when. Although incredibly informative in terms of signed language interpretation in court, yet again these studies have focused on interpreting for people who are accessing the justice system, in the form of witnesses, defendants, or complainants. Thus this pilot study is seminal, in that it is the first linguistic study to examine interpretation for deaf jurors in the court system.

Interpreting for Jurors

In the interpreting literature, very little consideration has been given to interpreting for jurors, as people are typically not eligible to serve as jurors if they cannot understand the language of the court. Non-English speaking people can now serve as jurors in the state of New Mexico in the United States (Montalvo, 2001). Additionally, deaf people in some states in the United States, and also in New Zealand, can serve as jurors, as it has been established that they are prevented from accessing the language of the court due to hearing loss, rather than the fact that they cannot use English.

There are different challenges for interpreters working with jurors, in that because the role of the client is different, the goal of the interpretation is also different (Mather & Mather, 2003; Montalvo, 2001). The role of a juror is

> to listen and accurately remember each piece of evidence, where necessary to draw inferences of fact from that evidence, using their experience of everyday life and at the same time evaluate the credibility of witnesses and the relative importance of evidence . . . to understand and apply directions individually and, when they retire as a jury, to collectively compare the facts with the contents of the judge's instruction on the law and arrive at a verdict. (Darbyshire, Maughan & Stewart, cited in NSWLRC, 2004, p. 17)

According to Findlay (1994), "In their role of fact-finder, the jurors should understand and weigh up the evidence presented, assess the credibility of witnesses and decide on the likelihood of certain events having occurred in the light of the jurors' personal experiences" (cited in NSWLRC, 2004, p. 13). Thus it can be seen, that as opposed to witnesses, defendants, or complainants who typically report their version of events, a juror has to make decisions based on the understanding and interpretation of information received. Therefore their information access needs are different.

Mather and Mather (2003) explored the needs of deaf jurors in receiving information via English/ASL interpreters, and evaluated whether this should occur through meaningful interpretations or through the verbatim transmission of information. In effect, they revisited the point raised in Brennan and Brown's (1997) work, acknowledging that interpreters need to borrow from English in order to convey legal concepts, terminology, and key facts of the case so that jurors can sufficiently access information for deliberation purposes. To date, no linguistic studies have been carried out on the efficacy of interpreting for the purposes of a deaf juror; confirming that this study is pioneering a new aspect of research on courtroom interpreting.

In addition to the analysis of interpretation accuracy and the evaluation of the effectiveness of English to Auslan interpretations in conveying information to deaf jurors, this study also focuses on juror comprehension. Very few studies have explored the actual comprehension of signed language interpretations generally (Napier & Rohan, 2007), let alone in court. Therefore key questions to be considered include: What do deaf jurors understand in court? How does that compare to hearing jurors? Is comprehension influenced by receiving the information directly or indirectly (via an interpreter)?

Juror and Legal Text Comprehension

In a recent interview in an Australian newspaper, the Hon. James Wood, QC expressed concern about how much lay people serving as jurors really understood (Dick, 2007). There have been several studies of the comprehension of legal texts, which have highlighted that even hearing people listening directly to spoken English can experience difficulty in comprehending legal texts, such as police cautions or jury instructions. For example, Cotterill (2000) found that the way that a police officer delivers a caution can influence its comprehensibility. Dumas (2000) asserted that jurors experience difficulty in understanding the syntactic and semantic complexities of jury instructions, and that any misunderstanding can be minimized through the use of standardized jury pattern instructions.

The seminal study on juror comprehension, however, was conducted by Charrow and Charrow (1979a; 1979b), which tested and proved the hypothesis that standard jury instructions are not well understood by most jurors. First, they identified a series of complex linguistic constructions in 14 standard jury instructions, which they hypothesized would be difficult to understand. Then they measured the comprehensibility of these instructions by administering a test, whereby jurors listened to these instructions and paraphrased their understanding of what the instructions meant. Charrow and Charrow then re-wrote the instructions, eliminating the problematic constructions, and re-tested the jurors. They found that the re-written instructions were better understood. Subsequent related studies have also confirmed that jury instructions fail to communicate central points of the law (Elwork, Sales, & Alfini, 1982; Hansen, Dirksen, Kuchler, Kunz, & Neumann, 2006; Luginbuhl, 1992; Steele & Thornburg, 1988).

A particularly interesting study is that of Judith Levi (1993), who conducted a linguistic evaluation of jury comprehension of instructions in her role as a linguistic expert witness. Levi analyzed and discussed the language of the Illinois Pattern Instructions (IPI), which are used in the sentencing phase of a murder trial, in order to assess how well the language used in these instructions served in its purpose to clearly communicate the legal concepts to the jury that they needed to understand for sentencing. The study served as a follow-up to a survey conducted by Zeisel (1990, cited in Levi, 1993), which concluded that a consistent majority of jurors misunderstood central points of law concerning deliberations on the death penalty, resulting in an increased likelihood that the jurors will impose the death penalty. Levi's linguistic analysis of the IPI also found:

- a consistent theme of presumption of death at all levels of the text (syntax, semantics, pragmatics, and discourse organization);[2]
- syntactical challenges, for example, use of multiple negatives, covert negatives, and embedded clauses;
- semantic ambiguity, for instance, use of the words "you" and "your finding" and whether this should be interpreted as a singular or group reference;
- incohesive discourse organization, that is, confusing sequencing of points, discontinuity, and needless interruptions to the flow with unrelated information;
- and pragmatic problems in that "jurors were given wholly insufficient information from which they had to deduce, or infer, a number of highly significant but regrettably obscured components of both federal and state law" (Levi, 1993, p. 31).

RESEARCH QUESTIONS

This research project sought to investigate deaf jurors' access to courtroom proceedings via interpreting. The key research questions were as follows

1. How translatable are legal concepts from English into Auslan?
2. How accurately are legal concepts and terminology interpreted from English into Auslan?
3. How much do hearing jurors comprehend of a judge's summation?

2. For example, "At one point . . . the judge first tells the jurors how to sentence the defendant to death and then how to give him a sentence that preserves his life—and then inexplicably restates how to sentence him to death. This death-life-death sequence clearly emphasizes the option of death, not only by repeating it twice but also by presenting it in the two most salient positions within a list, first and last" (Levi, 1993, p. 47).

4. How much do deaf jurors comprehend of a judge's summation?
5. Is there a significant difference between levels of comprehension between deaf and hearing jurors?
6. Are deaf jurors disadvantaged by relying on signed language interpreters to access information?
7. What are deaf and hearing jurors' perceptions of the content of the judge's summation?
8. What are deaf and hearing jurors' perceptions of jury duties?
9. What are Auslan/English interpreters' perceptions of interpreting for deaf jurors?
10. How effectively can deaf jurors' access courtroom proceedings via signed language interpreting?

METHODOLOGY

An experimental study was designed to replicate aspects of the courtroom experience. It was decided to test 12 would-be jurors, six deaf and six hearing, in order to compare their level of understanding of a legal text. The jurors were briefed with information as if they had been present throughout a trial, then were asked to respond to questions concerning two excerpts from a judge's summation taken from the end of a real court case. The goal of the study was to evaluate the accuracy of the interpretation from English into Auslan in relation to legal concepts, and to assess levels of comprehension of information received directly or indirectly through an interpreter. Given the small number of participants in the study, it should be emphasized that this study should only be considered as a pilot in preparation for a larger study.

Source Text

A judge's summation from a case that had been tried in the Supreme Court of NSW, Criminal Division, was selected by the NSWLRC. The case was *Regina v. Rodney Ivan Kerr,* which took place between October 27 and November 6, 2003. Rodney Ivan Kerr was charged with the manslaughter of William Christopher Harris at Redfern station in NSW. He was also charged with affray and endangering the safety of a person on the railway. Two excerpts were selected by representatives of the NSWLRC that incorporated sufficient legal terminology and important facts of the case. Excerpt 1 was from pages 14–27 of the summation and was delivered on Tuesday, November 4, 2003. Text 2 was from pages 99–107 of the summation and was delivered on Thursday, November 6, 2003.

Procedure

Two qualified Auslan/English interpreters were recruited to interpret the judge's summation from English into Auslan for recording on video. In order to approximate the level of background information interpreters would normally have if present throughout a real trial, both interpreters were provided with background materials, including a brief background to the case, a copy of the indictment, the first 14 pages of the transcribed summation prior to the first excerpt and the written directions referred to by the judge in the excerpts to be interpreted. These materials were provided two days prior to filming.

Two deaf participants were also recruited to attend the filming of the interpretation in order to provide a live audience for the interpreters. The interpreters were provided with the opportunity to discuss interpreting strategies and suggestions for Auslan signs with each other. They were then given time to discuss and agree on the signs to be used with their deaf audience. This would normally be the case in a real court situation. Signs were agreed upon for the following legal terms that came up throughout the text: accused, affray, assault, beyond reasonable doubt, director of public prosecutions, guilty, jury, manslaughter, parole, supreme court, verdict, and victim.

The member of the research team with legal experience acted as the judge and provided a short warm up reading to give interpreters the opportunity to become familiarized with the speaker's voice and pace of delivery, and the situation in general. Once filming commenced, the "judge" read the selected excerpt 1 as one interpreter carried out the interpretation simultaneously into Auslan and the second interpreter acted as prompt/support. This again simulates the procedure that would occur normally during a trial. Both the interpreter and the "judge" reading the source text were filmed.

A five-minute break was provided between the two selected excerpts and the same procedure was then followed for the second source text. For the purpose of minimizing disruption in such a short exercise, the same interpreter carried out the interpretation of the second excerpt.

On completion of the filming, the interpreters and deaf people participated in a debriefing separately with researchers. The interpreters were asked to comment on any challenges encountered, strategies used, differences to interpreting for deaf witnesses, defendants, or complainants, and any other general observations. The interpreters commented that there were some challenging parts of the text, especially in relation to use of legalese; and that the text felt repetitive. The interpreters were confident that they had met the needs of the deaf audience, but were conscious of the different strategies used to ensure that the jurors could access the terminology, for example, using more English mouthing and fingerspelling (i.e., borrowing).

The deaf people were asked to comment on anything they found difficult to understand, if they felt they could access courtroom proceedings through an interpreter sufficiently enough to serve as a juror, and any other general observations. Both commented that they felt that they had understood the interpretation clearly, and if serving as jurors would have felt able to make an informed decision about the guilt of the defendant. They both expressed interest to serve as jurors if it were made possible.

The next stage involved the translation of the filmed Auslan interpretation back into written English, which was conducted by a third interpreter who was not present during filming, and who was provided with the same background material and instructions as provided to other participants prior to the back translation task. The process of back translation was used in order to ensure reliability and content validity of the English to Auslan interpretation, and to identify any levels of mistranslation. Back translation is a method commonly used for verification of translated tests between spoken languages (Hambleton & De Jong, 2003; Hambleton & Patsula, 1999; Stansfield, 2003), and between spoken and signed languages (Cornes, Rohan, Napier, & Rey, 2006; Montoya et al., 2004). Key concepts were identified in the original summation and a content analysis was conducted of the back translation to identify the extent to which these concepts were accurately conveyed.

Drawing on the work of language testing experts (Brindley & Slatyer, 2002; Graessar, Mills, & Zwaan, 1997; Hughes, 1989; McNamara, 2000), two videos were produced for the comprehension test to ensure that participants would be tested in the same language as the source text they received (i.e., English or Auslan), and thus minimize differences in testing procedure for deaf and hearing participants. The first video, for deaf participants, was signed in Auslan by a researcher and consisted of the following sections:

- Introduction and overall instructions.
- Warm-up text consisting of the first 5 minutes of the judge's summation interpreted into Auslan.
- The two excerpts from the summation interpreted into Auslan.
- Instructions on the nature of the questions that will be asked and how participants were to respond.
- Twelve questions consisting of:
    - four true/false questions
    - four multiple choice questions
    - four open-ended questions.

All questions were repeated before a response was requested.

The Auslan interpretation of the warm up text and the two excerpts were presented as picture in picture, so that people would see the interpreter on screen, and the judge reading the summation in a smaller box on screen, to provide a visual link to the reading of the original text. The test was then piloted with one of the deaf people who had been present at the original filming. This person was asked to comment on the clarity of the instructions and questions in Auslan, and on the level of comfort at watching the interpreter and judge on the same screen. Once confirmed that the test was comprehensible, the actual data collection was arranged.

The video for the six hearing participants consisted of the same sections as the video for deaf participants. The warm-up text and the two excerpts from the summation shown to participants consisted only of the judge reading the original text. Instructions and questions for the comprehension component of the video were spoken to the camera by a researcher.

Two days prior to the test, deaf and hearing comprehension test participants were sent a brief background to the case and the written instructions provided to interpreters. Participants then attended the test venue individually and watched the relevant video and instructions. All participants were also provided with a written version of questions after they had watched the summation. All participants were filmed giving their responses orally or in Auslan to the camera. A researcher was present during this activity to pause the video for answers as required.

At the end of the comprehension test, all participants were also asked to comment on their experience and what they thought easier or more challenging in the task. Deaf participants, and hearing participants with no jury experience, were asked about their willingness to be involved in a jury in the future. Hearing participants with jury experience were asked to comment on how this activity compared to their past experience. All answers provided were then transcribed from videotape.

Participants

The interpreter who carried out the simultaneous interpretation of the source text into Auslan has been a professionally accredited interpreter since 1990. Although not a native signer, she has worked since 1986 as an interpreter in a variety of settings, and her legal interpreting experience includes murder and rape trials, family court, solicitor's appointments, and mental health tribunals. The interpreter also possessed tertiary qualifications, including a doctorate.

The interpreter acting as prompt to the simultaneous interpretation of the source text into Auslan has also been a professionally accredited interpreter since 1992. Although also not a native signer, she has worked since 1988 as an interpreter in a variety of contexts. In terms of legal settings, these include mentions and short trials within local, district, and supreme courts for both criminal and civil matters. The interpreter also possesses both undergraduate and postgraduate university qualifications.

Two deaf people attended the filming of the interpretation of the source text into Auslan. One deaf person was a native signer who is an Auslan dominant signer with some English skills. The other deaf person was a non-native signer who uses Auslan as her preferred method of communication, but has high literacy in English and considers herself to be bilingual. These two were chosen to represent two extremes of the Deaf community, so that the interpreters would pitch their interpretation to meet the needs of both audience members.

The interpreter who carried out the back translation of the interpreted text into English has been a professionally accredited interpreter since 1990. Although not a native Auslan user, her experience in legal interpreting spans court, mediation sessions, tribunals and hearings, police interviews, solicitor appointments, pre-trial conferences, and dispute resolution. In addition, she has worked as a paralegal advocate in a previous position as the manager of a community service.

Deaf and hearing participants for the comprehension test were recruited through the dissemination of a flyer throughout the university campus, and to contacts of the research team. The final group of jurors were twelve people (six deaf, six hearing) selected to provide a broad representation across the following variables: age, gender, highest educational attainment, employment category, and first language, as per the directions from the NSW Office of the Director for Public Prosecutions regarding jury selection (DPP, 2003). An attempt was made to include non-native users of Auslan and similarly non-native users of English in order to include the additional challenge experienced by such jurors. The characteristics of all the jurors can be seen in Table 1 and Table 2.

RESULTS AND DISCUSSION

Presented here are the results from a linguistic analysis of the source text, a content analysis of the source and back translated texts, the results of the comprehension test, and the post-test interviews.

Analysis of Source Text

A linguistic analysis of the original spoken English source text identified key issues that may have presented challenges to the interpreter. These included:

- The use of archaic expressions, for example, *three in number, element one will occasion you no difficulty,* and *a country blast on its horn.*
- An error in the oral reading of the written text resulting in a new 'source text.' In particular one example, where the phrase "the deliberate attack or attacks" was heard, which was a misreading of the phrase *deliberate act or acts.*
- Reference to other parties whose role in the trial was not explained and was not readily apparent from the context. For example, in the sentence "Mr. Button, I think, urged Mr. Mikulic as perhaps the most reliable"; Mr. Button was the barrister for the defendant, and Mr. Mikulic was one of the witnesses commenting on the distance between the defendant and victim at the train station. Although neither party was relevant to the questions that

TABLE 1. *Characteristics of Hearing Juror Participants*

		Participant					
		1	2	3	4	5	6
Variables	Gender	M	M	M	F	F	F
	Age range	18–30	31–49	50+	18–30	31–49	50+
	Highest educational attainment	Tertiary (TAFE)	Higher School certificate	Tertiary (TAFE)	Tertiary (TAFE)	Tertiary (university)	School certificate
	Employment category	Manual/Trade/ Paraprofessional	White collar/ professional	White collar/ professional	White collar/ professional	White collar/ professional	White collar/ professional
	First language	English	Italian	English	English	Korean	English

TABLE 2. *Characteristics of Deaf Juror Participants*

		Participant					
		1	2	3	4	5	6
Variables	Gender	M	M	M	F	F	F
	Age range	18–30	31–49	50+	18–30	31–49	50+
	Highest educational attainment	Tertiary (university)	Tertiary (TAFE)	Tertiary (TAFE)	Tertiary (university)	Higher School certificate	School certificate
	Employment category	White collar/ professional	Manual/Trade/ Paraprofessional	Manual/Trade/ Paraprofessional	White collar/ professional	Not in workforce (student)	Manual/Trade/ Paraprofessional
	First language	English	Auslan	Auslan	English	Auslan	Auslan

were asked in the comprehension test, the inclusion of this information placed additional cognitive strain on the interpreters and the participants who naturally are attempting to create links between the information they are being provided with.
- Unclear use of pronouns, for example, with reference to the CCTV camera photographic evidence, the judge states "For instance, photograph number 3, by which time the train is in and people are getting off, you may think Mr. Kerr and his group is getting off, photograph 3 is at 12.45 and 37 seconds, and then at 12.46 and 5 seconds is Exhibit E, the one with **his** hands on the platform, a split second before the train hit **him**." In the final clause, the pronouns "his" and "him" do not refer to the defendant Mr. Kerr, but in fact to the victim Mr. Christopher.
- Clear examples of legalese, for example, the use of the term *reasonable and proportionate.* As the judge says himself, "It is not suggested that there is any distinction between those two words, reasonable or proportionate. They are embodying essentially the same concept which is a concept of reasonableness." Yet both terms are used throughout the text. This forces the interpreter to either reduce both terms to one Auslan sign or to use two Auslan signs that convey exactly the same meaning but in a different form in order to match the form of the English text.

Analysis of Interpretation

An analysis of the English to Auslan interpretation yielded unsurprising results. As per Brennan and Brown's (1997) study of BSL/English interpreters, the interpreter was found to use a literal translation style—using mouthing and/or fingerspelling to borrow terms from English, especially legal concepts. An example can be seen in Figure 1 where the interpreter can be seen to accompany the mouthing of the phrase 'grevious bodily harm' with fingerspelling (the transcription depicts signs used in captialised letters, and English mouthing is illustrated in the words above the line).

Content Analysis of Source Text and Back Translation

The source text was analyzed to identify the key legal concepts presented in the summation and the extent these were accurately inter-

Original spoken English source:

Broadly, to prove murder the Crown must establish two things. The first is that the death of the victim was caused by the acts of the accused, and the second is they must prove that in carrying out these acts the accused person had a particular state of mind, that is, he intended to kill the victim or he intended to cause that victim very serious bodily injury, what is called by the lawyers grievous bodily harm.

Auslan interpretation:

for	prove	murder	solicitor	must	prove	two things	first	that
FOR	PROVE	MURDER	SOLICITOR	MUST	PROVE	TWO ONE-TWO	FIRST	PRO-1

person	die	happen	because of that	accused person	his behavior	second
PERSON	DIE	HAPPEN	WHY	PRO-2 PERSON	THEIR BEHAVIOR//	SECOND

Prove	what	that	person	behavior	before	plan	want
PROVE	WHAT?	PRO-2 PERSON	BEHAVIOR	WILFUL	BEFORE	PLAN	WANT

to kill	that	person	that	person	plan	want	kill	him
KILL PRO-1	PRO-1 WELL	PRO-2 PERSON	THINK	PLAN	YES	WANT	KILL	PRO-1

or	want	hurt	that person	serious	bodily	harm	called
OR	WANT	HURT	PRO-1	SERIOUS	BODY	HARM	QUOTATION-MARKERS

grievous	bodily	harm	gbh
G-R-I-E-V-O-U-S	BODY	H-A-R-M	G-B-H WELL

FIGURE 1. *Example of literal translation*

preted. Eight broad legal concepts were identified in the summation and have been summarized as follows:

1. Defining "manslaughter."
2. The first element of manslaughter.
   The second element of manslaughter.
3. Test of "causation."
4. Defining "reasonable and proportionate."
5. Clarifying the written directions—what did the accused do?
6. Clarifying the written directions—did the accused's actions give rise to a well-founded apprehension of physical harm?
7. Clarifying the written directions—was it reasonable for the victim to seek to escape?
8. Clarifying the written directions—was the method of escape reasonable and proportionate?

Within the above list of concepts, a number of other requirements were also identified that were used to assess the degree to which the live interpretation was accurate. A comparison of the broad legal concepts in the original text and the back translation text found that concepts 2 and 4 were translated accurately while concepts 1, 3, 5, 6, 7 and 8 raised issues ranging in severity from a change in the order of explanation to more significant changes in meaning. It is interesting to note that the analysis found the back translation of concept 4 to be superior to the original summation.

In terms of equivalence of content, analysis showed that the interpretation was 87.5% accurate. This was calculated based on the prevalence of 72 key legal concepts in the original source text, of which 63 were found in the back translation text. Figure 2 shows an example of equivalent concepts from the first paragraph of the first excerpt of the summation.

The purpose of analyzing the back translation was to assess the degree to which important concepts in the original summation were translated. In doing so, a note of caution must also be raised. The usual method for such an analysis, as used here, is to conduct a back translation from the target language (Auslan) to the source language (English) in order to see the degree to which there has been any shift in meaning. Although conducted by a qualified Auslan/English interpreter, there is still the potential for meaning to shift during the back translation process. It could be argued that even the reading of the original English text will introduce the potential for something to be misread or emphasis to

Source Text Version

> Let me move from that to the first count, that of manslaughter, and in order to explain the elements of the charge, and what the Crown must prove to establish manslaughter, it may assist if I very briefly, and I hope I do not confuse you, say a word about murder and the contrast between murder and manslaughter. You would appreciate, of course, there is no question in this trial of murder. Broadly, to prove murder the Crown must establish two things. The first is that the death of the victim was caused by the acts of the accused , and the second is they must prove that in carrying out these acts the accused person had a particular state of mind, that is, he intended to kill the victim or he intended to cause that victim very serious bodily injury , what is called by the lawyers grievous bodily harm .
> **(9 legal concepts)**

Back Translation

> Now moving on, I would like to talk about the first count on the indictment—manslaughter. I want to explain what this count entails and what the Crown must prove in order for you to be satisfied of the accused's guilt. Whilst I think it will be useful to provide you with some information, I'll direct the jury only very briefly as I don't want to confuse you. I want to clarify that manslaughter and murder are very different under the law. You of course would understand that in this trial we are not discussing a charge of murder. In regard to proving murder, the Crown would have to prove two elements. Firstly, that a person died as a result of the direct actions of an accused person; but also that the accused had formed an intention to kill that person. So there is a deliberate or intentional act that has caused that death or has caused serious harm to the person. Causing serious harm to the person is known as " grievous bodily harm ."
> **(7 legal concepts)**

FIGURE 2. *Example of equivalent concept*

be altered from that originally intended by the author. The legal concepts identified in the original text will now be examined.

KEY LEGAL CONCEPT 1— DEFINING "MANSLAUGHTER"

The issue of the difference between murder and manslaughter, that being the *mens rea* or intention to commit a crime, was accurately translated. However, the "reasonable person" test was not well translated. The summation clearly directed the jury to consider "the measure of responsibility being that of a reasonable person stepping off a train at Redfern." The back translation stated, "You can however make a decision about his words, language, his behavior." Although, the use of the word "objectively" was used in the very next sentence, it is uncertain if the average juror would understand the term "objectively" without the use of the example of the reasonable person. This therefore appears to be a problem with this part of the translation.

KEY LEGAL CONCEPT 2—THE FIRST AND SECOND ELEMENTS OF MANSLAUGHTER

No problems were identified with the translation of the first element of manslaughter. However, in relation to the second element of manslaughter, a subtle difference was identified between the summation referring to acts that "caused the death" of the victim compared with the back translation which refers to acts that "contributed to the death" of the victim. An act or acts that contribute to someone's death is different to an act or acts that cause someone's death. The accused may have contributed to the death but his act may not have caused the death.

KEY LEGAL CONCEPT 3—TEST OF "CAUSATION"

A major problem was identified in relation to the translation of this concept. The summation clearly left the interpretation of the evidence to the jury: "So that even if you were to find that the deceased himself, by his actions, contributed to his own death . . ."; whereas the back translation made an assumption about the interpretation of the evidence: "The deceased himself by his own conduct of getting onto the tracks clearly contributed to the final result of death. . . ." A judge never tells the jury how to interpret evidence. The jury is called "the tribunal of fact" because their job is to establish whether the facts, established by the evidence, support the charge. The judge is the "tribunal of law" and determines questions of law that help the jury in its job of only assessing admissible evidence. The back translation would indicate to the deaf juror that the judge has already decided this issue and therefore, the jury should follow suit.

KEY LEGAL CONCEPT 4—DEFINING "REASONABLE AND PROPORTIONATE"

The back translation was found to be better, in terms of plain English, than the summation. A minor comment could be made that the summation asks the jurors to consider first if there was a threat at all: "It is an objective view based upon what the deceased did in response to the threat made to him, if you find that there was such a threat"; whereas the back translation assumed there was a threat, although admittedly, the language is not conclusive.

KEY LEGAL CONCEPT 5—CLARIFYING THE WRITTEN DIRECTIONS: WHAT DID THE ACCUSED DO?

The summation leaves the question of whether the accused caused the death of the victim to the jury. The judge goes close to commenting on the truth of the evidence but ultimately leaves it to the jury by opining: "I do not think it is in the least controversial . . ."; whereas the back translation states on this issue: "All would agree that the victim was directly targeted . . ." This important difference is the difference in leaving facts for the jury to determine and the judge directing the jury on accepted facts—accepted by him and by implication the jury.

KEY LEGAL CONCEPT 6—CLARIFYING THE WRITTEN DIRECTIONS: DID THE ACCUSED'S ACTIONS GIVE RISE TO A WELL-FOUNDED APPREHENSION OF PHYSICAL HARM?

The order of the translation was found to be problematic. The following sentence, "In considering the victim's reaction and his sense of fear, was the person himself the kind of person that would experience trepidation more than any other reasonable person?" should have appeared towards the end of this part of the text, not midway through. It confuses the subjective with the objective test. The summation was deemed to be in the correct order. This did not appear to be hugely damaging because the objective test is clarified but it did cause some degree of confusion.

KEY LEGAL CONCEPT 7—CLARIFYING THE WRITTEN DIRECTIONS: WAS IT REASONABLE FOR THE VICTIM TO SEEK TO ESCAPE?

The back translation used the word "causally," which was assessed to be incorrect. This was not thought to be hugely damaging but confusing as the issue of well-founded apprehension of fear is not determinative alone of the issue of causation—it merely contributes to the issue of the presence of causation. Otherwise, there appear to be no other problems with the translation.

KEY LEGAL CONCEPT 8—CLARIFYING THE WRITTEN DIRECTIONS: WAS THE METHOD OF ESCAPE REASONABLE AND PROPORTIONATE?

A reference to the victim escaping because of a "weakness in character" was deemed to be an incorrect insertion, as it was not mentioned in the original summation. This is an objective test, not an assessment of the victim's character as to whether it was reasonable to escape the threat posed by the accused. Otherwise, no other problems were evident.

Thus, from the analysis of the back translation, it can be seen that there were some problems with translations of the broad legal concepts central to the case. Yet, the problems were largely subtle shifts between legal definitions or objectively presented facts to interpretations of the meaning of such statements.

Comprehension of Source Texts

The results of the comprehension test show that both hearing and deaf jurors misunderstood some concepts. In relation to the closed/multiple choice questions, approximately 10.5% of the questions were answered incorrectly by all participants. Of the open-ended questions, some responses were problematic from both deaf and hearing participants. Table 3 summarizes the correct responses by participants undertaking the comprehension task.

There is a minor difference, percentage-wise, between the number of correct responses from deaf and hearing participants (2.8% difference). Of all the errors in responses to true/false and multiple-choice questions, almost half (5 of 9 errors made) related to question 5, a multiple choice

TABLE 3. *Summary of Correct Responses Grouped by the Format of the Question*

Questions		Correct responses Deaf participants (n = 6)	Hearing participants (n = 6)	TOTAL (n =12)
True/false	Q1	6	6	12
	Q2	6	6	12
	Q3	6	6	12
	Q4	3	5	8
Multiple choice	Q5	3	5	8
	Q6	6	6	12
	Q7	6	5	11
	Q8	6	6	12
Open ended	Q9	6	4	10
	Q10	1	0	1
	Q11	5	6	11
	Q12	0	1	1
TOTAL		54/72 75%	56/72 77.8%	110/144 76.4%

question that was also the longest of all questions asked. Due to the small number of participants, however, this difference cannot be analyzed in terms of statistical significance.

A number of similarities can be seen in the responses made by deaf and hearing participants and in the errors seen in questions 4, 5, 10, and 12 in particular, suggesting that these items may have been challenging regardless of language used or whether the information was received directly or mediated through an interpreter. Table 4 provides the different open-ended responses to question 9 (the majority of which were correct), and question 10 (the majority of which were incorrect).

Interestingly, it can be seen in response to question 9, that all the deaf participants answered correctly, whereas two of the hearing respondents'

TABLE 4. *Responses to Q9 and Q10*

Participant	Question 9: Explain what witnesses said the two women with Mr Kerr did.	Question 10: Explain the legal rule of "causation"
	Correct answer: One or both women physically restrained Mr. Kerr. When Mr. Kerr broke free they again grabbed him and held him back.	*Correct answer: Did the accused's conduct cause the victim to die? It doesn't have to be the sole or effective cause but did the act or acts of the acts of the accused significantly or substantially contribute to the death of the victim.*
	Participant responses (correct/ incorrect)	
Deaf 1	Both women tried to restrain the man, to stop him from fighting with the other man. The man resisted and broke free, going for the other man. Both women again tried to hold the man but he went for the other man. What happened after that I don't know. (✓)	Sorry, I can't give an answer. (X)
Deaf 2	Witnesses saw the two women get off the train with Mr. Kerr. When Mr. Kerr became aggressive and approached the other man, the women pulled him back to stop him approaching him. Also, when Mr. Harris escaped by jumping onto the tracks, one women yelled 'look train coming.' That's what happened. (✓)	Causation. Two things, A and B happen. If A happens, then eventually B will happen. If A doesn't happen, maybe B would never happen. But if A happens B will definitely happen. (X)
Deaf 3	The two women tried to hold Mr.Kerr, then he broke free and ran up to the other man. The two women again grabbed him and held onto him. (✓)	What the accused made the victim do. (X)

continued

TABLE 4. *Continued*

Deaf 4	Witnesses said that the two women tried to restrain the man but he broke free so they grabbed him a second time to stop him approaching the victim. (✓)	Sorry, I don't know. (X)
Deaf 5	When the man got off the train the man started to yell at him. The two women tried to stop him but he continued so the women held him but he was determined and resisted. (✓)	Causation. The cause. The man was yelling and that made the other man fearful and run away. This was caused by his yelling at the victim. (X)
Deaf 6	The two women tried to help and keep the men separated, to hold onto the accused. (✓)	That means that the death happened because of the behaviour of the accused, causing the victim to die. There was a link. (✓)
Hearing 1	They went over to the victim and pinned him down. Held him down for a little while. (✓)	It goes back to the cause and effect. Was what the accused did, it's hard to put into words, was what the accused, did it cause the victim's action . . . what the accused did is the cause to the victim's action. And it has to be proved beyond reasonable doubt that one affected the other. (X)
Hearing 2	The two women got off the train with Mr. Kerr and as Mr. Kerr shouted at Mr. Harris they attempted to restrain him and hold him back. (✓)	Causation is cause and effect. If there is a consequence of an action and it can be proven that it is a reasonable response to the action of the accused, and the accused is said to have caused that response in the victim. If that victim is of firm mind and sound judgment then that is reasonable cause to say that the action of the accused caused that response in the victim. And it must be continuous. (X)

Hearing 3	They tried to stop Mr. Kerr. (X)	It's like cause and affect. A causes B there is causation there if A's act or saying causes B, there is a rule of causation in that incident. (X)
Hearing 4	The two women held Mr. Kerr back. (✓)	I was listening but causation and everything else . . . Cause of something that has happened but being able to prove that you intended something to happen and you were the reason for why it happened. (X)
Hearing 5	Mmmm nothing. They didn't do anything. Failed! (Laughs) Looking at my notes but . . . got off the train . . . yelled . . sorry. (X)	Hmm. It's the actual cause of it? I didn't write it all down but I understood there the question of cause in a common sense non-technical way. Determining criminal responsibility for serious criminal offences. That's what I would take it as. (X)
Hearing 6	When Mr. Kerr started yelling and saying 'what the f**k are you doing' or 'what the f**k are you looking at,' witnesses said the two women restrained Mr. Kerr. He escaped from their restraint, obviously it didn't appear it was a very strong restraint, they then went to restrain him again and he allowed himself to remain under constraint by the two women. (✓)	From my understanding as described here causation is an unbroken chain of cause and affect. If there is any break in that link between a particular cause and a particular effect, that is not legal causation. There can be several links in that chain but they have to be unbroken and they have to be related to one another. (✓)

answers were inaccurate or incomplete. It is also interesting to note that in question 9, the deaf participants' responses are more detailed, as compared to question 10 where the hearing participants provided fuller answers. This pattern was reversed for questions 11 and 12, where the hearing participants had a higher number of correct responses.

An overall pattern that can be seen in the responses to the comprehension test is the difference between responses to questions of fact and questions relating to legal concepts. Overall, most respondents answered questions of fact correctly. In the case of deaf respondents, this means that the facts of the case had been interpreted clearly and correctly and had been understood by deaf participants. When asked to comment on the comprehension test, four participants specifically mentioned the facts of the case as being one of the easier aspects of the activity.

When factual errors did arise, they sometimes arose in respondents who otherwise provided correct answers to more complex questions. An example of this can be seen in question 9. All the deaf respondents provided correct answers as to the accused being physically restrained by the women while only four of the hearing respondents provided a correct answer. One hearing respondent answered the question correctly but drew a conclusion as to the intentions of the accused to free himself from the grasp of the women. First, this response was not asked for by the activity but offered up by the respondent and second, it is inconclusive in terms of the accuracy of the conclusion drawn. One hearing respondent failed to answer the question and guessed incorrectly, yet this respondent had previously answered all of the questions about the legal concepts and the factual matrix correctly.

A similar pattern can be found with question 11, where one deaf respondent answered with "I can't remember what actual words he used but I remember he yelled. What he actually said I missed." This was an interesting response given the colorful language used by the accused and recounted accurately by the judge in his summation. Further, given that 11 other respondents recounted the wording almost verbatim, it is odd that one respondent missed it completely. It is unlikely that modesty is the reason for this respondent missing the words as the words can be changed when recounted so that they are not so offensive.

A possible explanation for this observation is that the facts of the case were sparsely distributed in the body of the text, often arising incidentally within a discussion about a legal concept. These facts were also rarely repeated during the excerpts selected for this study, therefore making them easier to miss. This suggests that in an actual trial, where evidence is presented over a longer period of time and in a more systematic manner, these comprehension errors may decrease as jurors would have had time to absorb evidence and arguments before hearing the judge's summation.

Discussion will now turn to responses to questions where a pattern of misunderstanding may be found. Five out of six hearing respondents answered question 4 correctly with one additional respondent giving the correct answer but being confused by the reference to murder, stating that the summation had been addressing the issue of manslaughter. Only three out of the six deaf respondents answered this question correctly however, with one of the respondents who answered correctly admitting they did not understand the interpretation of the phrase "beyond reasonable doubt." When the researcher simplified this to "without doubt," the respondent confirmed their correct answer. Overall this may indicate a low level understanding of a basic threshold concept in the trial of criminal law cases. If respondents cannot grasp this basic threshold concept then the rest of the evidence may well be lost or misinterpreted by the jury, whether hearing or deaf, in the jury room. However, the level of misunderstanding is comparable between the two sample groups meaning that the concept or the form of the question were difficult for both groups. This issue will be discussed further below.

Turning to responses to question 5, only one of the hearing respondents answered this question incorrectly compared to three of the deaf respondents. This response is a concern as this question is a threshold question that distinguishes between the two elements of murder that is the *mens rea* (the intention to kill) and the *actus reus* (the act of killing). The prosecution has the burden to prove beyond a reasonable doubt that the accused intended to kill the victim or acted with reckless indifference to human life and did physically kill the victim. If deaf jurors have difficulty understanding the difference between the act and the intention to kill then there is the potential for juries to deliver unsafe verdicts.

It should also be noted that question 5 was also the longest of the questions asked of the participants. This raises the challenge of modality in the design of comprehension materials (Hughes, 1989). In this study this becomes an issue not only for participants responding to complex verbal information, but also signed multiple choice items which must also be held in memory as the participant assesses the question, the options and their recollections.

Questions 10 and 12 resulted in the highest number of errors. Almost all of the hearing respondents answered question 10 incorrectly. Most were close to the correct answer but none of the hearing respondents stated the rule correctly. Whether this is fatal to their ultimate understanding of the concept and would lead to an unsafe verdict is hard to tell. The following elements of the responses of hearing respondents show how close the responses were to the correct answer:

- "did what the accused do cause the victim's action"?
- "the accused is said to have caused the response in the victim"
- "if A's act or saying causes B"
- "cause of something happening"
- "it's the actual cause of it"
- "an unbroken chain of cause and effect"

In a result that is arguably better than the hearing respondents, one deaf respondent correctly answered the question. This respondent stated, "the death happened because of the behavior of the accused, causing the victim to die. There was a link." While this response is not perfect in relation to the events establishing an unbroken chain of events, it is the best and most accurate response from the entire sample. The other five deaf respondents made the following responses in part:

- "sorry I can't give an answer"
- "if A happens, then eventually B will happen"
- "what the accused caused the victim to do"
- "sorry I don't know"
- "the man was yelling and that made the other man fearful and run away"

Turning to question 12, only one hearing respondent gave a correct account of the "reasonable and proportionate response." Three respondents correctly pointed out that the victim's response needed to be reasonable compared to the risk posed by the accused for causation to be made out. The remaining two hearing respondents totally missed the point and answered the question by talking about irrelevant facts.

All of the deaf respondents answered the question incorrectly. The closest deaf respondent stated, "We need to think about what is fair and proportionate." The respondent in question did not go on to explain what they meant by "fair" and "proportionate." We may assume that "proportionate" meant whether the victim's response was proportionate to the threat by the accused. However, "fair" probably does not mean invoking the objective test. It is too easy for a respondent to not understand the difference between the subjective test ("fair" as judged by the victim's demeanor) and the objective test ("fair" as judged by the reasonable person). It is the lack of adequate explanation that makes even this response an incorrect answer. Only two of the deaf respondents raised the element of reasonableness. The other three deaf respondents totally missed the point and talked about the facts, as did the two above mentioned hearing respondents.

Again, this is a complex legal concept that is difficult to grasp but an important concept that effectively proves the causation issue so central to a successful manslaughter charge. The high level of misunderstanding by both hearing and deaf respondents is a concern.

Post-test Interviews

In the post-test interviews, all participants commented that the facts were easy to follow, but that the legalistic language and amount of repetition made the text difficult to comprehend. Figure 3 gives examples of deaf and hearing responses to the question "What was harder or easier to understand?"

Although the interpreters had agreed on the signs to be used with the deaf audience at the time of filming, there were comments from two of the deaf comprehension test participants about the choice of signs, as seen in Figure 4.

This is typical of the lexical sociolinguistic variation in Auslan, where different signs are used according to regional, dialectical, and age differences (Johnston & Schembri, 2007). This is one of the limitations of using a pre-recorded video test. If the interpreter had been in a courtroom with the two deaf people who made these comments, obviously she would have discussed and agreed to use the signs that they use. Nonetheless, the preference for alternative signs from two deaf participants did not seem to impair their comprehension of the content.

Those hearing participants, who had previously served as jury members, were asked to compare their participation in the comprehension test with their prior experience. This question was asked in order to ascertain the realism of the test, thus validating the credibility of the results.[3] Figure 5 outlines some of their responses.

3. One of the hearing participants had prior experience in court, but as a Korean-English interpreter not a jury member; so this was discounted.

Deaf responses

I didn't understand what was involved in court proceedings before. I was surprised about the repetition. I understood the interpreter, yes, but the language used . . . that I knew I had to try to remember. I understood everything the interpreter signed, that was very easy and clear. She was clear about who did what, she created the context, so it was easy to understand who did what. That made it easy to understand. The only difficulty was the legal language like 'beyond reasonable doubt.' I know it's legal language. Words like 'affray.' So you have to remember these things. And they get repeated, over and over. A bit boring!

What really helped me was the use of space, the explanation in Auslan. Before I arrived I didn't know the signs for manslaughter, for example so having the interpreter explain the sign for the word helped me. Without that it would have gone over my head. What was more difficult was the pace. It was fast so you didn't have time to sit back and take it in. It started easier and then got more complex.

Hearing responses

The easier parts were the facts because it was quite a simple scenario other than when the women appeared because there was not mention of them getting off the train with Mr. Kerr so that was really odd. The harder part was the language used in law. And the guy was just reading off and there seemed to be a lot of repeating so you almost get lost in it. It's almost more understandable if you just say this is this, this is this. Which is probably why the fact part of it is easier for me. When you start to repeat things, it becomes a little muddled.

Coming from a different cultural and language background [Korean] I had to concentrate on it all the time but I found it the judge tried to explain everything very clearly but the wordy explanations sometimes caused not confusion but made it even harder for me to follow what he was trying to say. Because it was all written in legal expressions if it was written in common newspaper language or more everyday language it might be more clearly understandable but it is a legal document and as the judge said without adding or deleting any information delivering the message accurately was not very easy for all parties . . . I could follow especially with the written documents but without this I would have to focus more to follow what he said.

FIGURE 3. *What was harder or easier to understand*

Alternatively, hearing participants with no previous jury service were asked to comment on how confident they felt about being a juror after their brief experience in this study. Their responses can be seen in Figure 6.

I think I understood things without too much difficulty. The interpreter's signing was a little unusual, for example signing DOUBT NOTHING. I prefer DOUBT DON'T-HAVE

I think I needed more explanation in Auslan about some of the terms and their meaning. For example, 'beyond reasonable doubt.' I don't think the interpretation used was right—DOUBT NOTHING. I think more explanation was needed. The other thing was the sign 'guilty.' I use this sign GUILTY (small finger tapped on chest) [rather than sign used by interpreter which was repetition of the fingerspelled letter G]. So a few things could have been clearer. But otherwise I followed things easily, especially the description of what happened. But the terms used, that was a bit harder.

FIGURE 4. *Comments about choice of signs*

As deaf people cannot currently serve as jurors in NSW, we could not ask them to compare their experiences. However, we did ask them how they would feel about being a juror, in light of this research participation experience. Figure 7 illustrates the comments they made.

Although anecdotally it seems that people typically attempt to get out of jury duty, it is worthy of note that the deaf people involved in this study would like the opportunity to carry out their civic duty, and participate in the judicial system on an equal footing with hearing people. The final question that we asked the deaf participants was "In order to have equal access, what would you need as a deaf juror (other than an interpreter)?" Their thoughts are revealed in Figure 8.

It was similar and those points the judge was explaining did happen in the real case I was in. I guess it was harder here just coming into it in the middle and not having time to go and reflect. I did actually take notes in the real case which I didn't here today which that does help me to work things out in my mind a bit better. I think if I was deciding the fate of some for the next 10 years I would take notes. Just being on your own, I know you are meant to make up your own mind but in the jury room I did find there was that talk amongst yourselves and people who had more divergent views did come to see things more from the same point of view. And going back over statements and photographs and exhibits.

Yes definitely [it was an easier experience]. I suppose when you've been through the whole 3 or 4 days I was a bit over it whereas I really listened to this. It was just so much clearer.

FIGURE 5. *Comparisons with prior juror experience (hearing participants)*

Can't say I'm looking forward to it but if I do it, it won't be a problem. It needs to be done and I'm happy to do it . . . It's part of modern day society. This is how we've structured our law reforms and this is what you have to do so it's fine. It's not something I would choose to avoid doing.

Don't think I would ever feel confident about being a member of a jury because I feel like it is a lot of responsibility trying to work out what is what if someone is guilty, certain acts. I guess being able to take in all the information, and trying to remember it. I guess you would have it documented as well and I guess you would probably find it a bit disturbing knowing certain things but (not pleasant things) yes, I would do it and I would probably feel alright doing but it is a big responsibility trying to work out someone's fate.

This would have only taken a week say, but that would still have been a week of intense concentration, keeping facts straight, your notes together would have helped, if you're a juror without access to notes, access to written material, you are just sitting there sucking it all in getting the feel of the case and when it came time to deliberate, it would be easy for anybody without notes to forget significant points or to misinterpret those points . . . I could participate and hopefully come up with the verdict. These types of explanations are very helpful [referring to the written directions]. We might know the word but not know how to elaborate on the complete definition in law, and an understanding of terms and phrases.

FIGURE 6. *Thoughts about being a juror (hearing)*

CONCLUSION

Regardless of the information provided to participants prior to undertaking the various stages of this study, the source text was still decontextualized from an actual court case and the gradual introduction of material that would have occurred in a real life case. The material was also challenging as hearing "jurors" equally misunderstood some aspects of the summation even though they were receiving the information directly in English. In a real life courtroom, jurors would have had time to absorb evidence and arguments before the hearing judge's summation. Even with these limitations, and the fact that the study had a small sample size, this research has demonstrated that:

- legal facts and concepts can be translated into Auslan;
- Auslan interpreting can provide effective access to court proceedings for a deaf juror—but certain conditions are necessary;

I would love to be involved if I had the opportunity. I would be interested to hear about what happened, the victim and other person's arguments. I think it would be a good experience. I watch television and think that it would be interesting to find out what really happened.

I've been asked to be on a jury twice but I've had to say that I couldn't because I am deaf. I think it would be interesting to be involved. I know it can be boring, heavy work but I know it is the duty of the community to judge their peers. In this situation I felt I could participate but there was one thing about the three charges: it was hard for me to see, if we said not guilty to the first charge, how we would then decide on the remaining two charges. That wasn't really clear to me—the difference between charge 2 and 3. I know that it may be because it was the middle of the case—maybe there was more in depth discussion that had been held about the difference between charges 2 and 3 or if they made a decision about not being guilty on the first charge then we would look more in depth at charges 2 or 3.

Yes, because if I could, I would. I've never done it before so I would want to.

Yes, because we need to be equal with the hearing community. Deaf people are excluded from so many things. I got a letter asking me to go for jury duty and I would have loved to but I knew that because I am deaf I had to sign the form and say that I couldn't attend because I am Deaf. I feel I want to be involved because it is right for society.

At first no, but this experience was interesting. I felt scared before that. I didn't want to do it but having watched this I thought I could be involved. But maybe not a murder trial that would be intimidating but something more straightforward . . . One thing is that deaf people vary in their skill and their education. That worries me a bit. We need to be careful about saying if someone is guilty or innocent. They could be sent to jail for something they haven't done. But then, that's the same for hearing people.

I think it would be interesting and I would want to be seen as equal. With an interpreter, I would be fine. I don't see any issues. And if the opportunity arises in the future, I might try to take it.

FIGURE 7. *Thoughts about being a juror (deaf)*

- hearing people misunderstood court proceedings without being disadvantaged by hearing loss;
- deaf people are willing and able to serve as jurors.

To conclude, we revisit and respond to each of the research questions posed earlier in Figure 9.

I think you would need an interpreter like [Interpreter name]. A level 2 [NAATI paraprofessional] interpreter wouldn't be skilled enough. They would need to be level 3 [NAATI professional], fluent and experienced in court work. Before I came here today, I was thinking that the juror and the interpreter would need to have a good relationship. Without a good relationship, the process wouldn't work so well.

I don't know if it is usual for jurors to have access to notes every day, to later consider what was said. That would be worth having. I don't think I would need a video (of the interpreter). I think that is all. Access to what the [rest of the] jury has.

An interpreter as you said, and papers that I could read before or through the trial especially if the interpreter wasn't clear. That would be useful.

Yes an interpreter but also I need to know how the court runs everything. One way would be for notes that I could take home to read—to make sure that I understand before I go in on the first day. Sometimes at the start, on the first day there is so much to understand so knowing why we are there, the parties, what happened, that would be good to know in advance.

First, education and an explanation of basic terminology. Second, basic awareness of how the court works and how we need to behave. For example, should we allow our emotions to be involved or be detached. We need to understand how to separate out issues and what to set aside, like emotions. I think it is important and that will build our confidence and help us to make the right decision.

FIGURE 8. *Access needs for deaf jurors*

1. How translatable are legal concepts from English into Auslan?
2. How accurately are legal concepts and terminology interpreted from English into Auslan?
3. How much do hearing jurors comprehend of a judge's summation?
4. How much do deaf jurors comprehend of a judge's summation?
5. Is there a significant difference between levels of comprehension between deaf and hearing jurors?
6. Are deaf jurors disadvantaged by relying on sign language interpreters to access information?
7. What are deaf and hearing jurors' perceptions of the content of the judge's summation?
8. What are deaf and hearing jurors' perceptions of jury duties?
9. What are Auslan/English interpreters' perceptions of interpreting for deaf jurors?
10. How effectively can deaf jurors' access courtroom proceedings via sign language interpreting?

FIGURE 9. *Research questions*

We found that:

1. Legal concepts are translatable from English into Auslan, but interpreters need to be careful not to skew the legal definitions or to bias the text with subtle shifts in the interpretation.
2. In this study, we found that the legal concepts and terminology present in the original judge's summation were generally interpreted from English into Auslan accurately, with 87.5% accuracy.
3. Hearing jurors in this study answered almost 78% of the comprehension test questions correctly, implying a relatively high level of comprehension of the judge's summation.
4. Deaf jurors in this study answered 75% of the comprehension test questions correctly, implying a relatively high level of comprehension of the judge's summation.
5. The findings of this study demonstrate that levels of comprehension between deaf and hearing jurors were similar.
6. Thus, it appears that deaf jurors in this study were not disadvantaged by relying on signed language interpreters to access information in court.
7. Deaf and hearing jurors in this particular study similarly perceived the content of the judge's summation to be complex and repetitive.
8. Deaf and hearing jurors regarded jury service as a necessary civic duty. The deaf jurors all expressed interest in serving as jurors if they were afforded the opportunity.
9. The Auslan/English interpreters' in this study did note a difference in interpreting for deaf jurors (as compared to deaf witnesses, defendants, etc.), but felt confident that they could adequately service their information needs.
10. The findings of this pilot study suggest that the small number of deaf jurors involved could effectively access courtroom proceedings via signed language interpreting.

RECOMMENDATIONS

- That deaf people be permitted to serve as jurors in criminal cases in NSW, with access provided through a team of interpreters, and additional support through the provision of written documents in advance and access to a transcript at the end of each trial day.

- That deaf people serving as jurors must have reasonable competence in English (as does any juror), in order to understand the English legal terms when they are borrowed into Auslan by interpreters (via fingerspelling and/or mouthing), and to understand any written materials.
- Only experienced legal interpreters should work with deaf jurors and they should be qualified at National Accreditation Authority for Translators and Interpreters (NAATI) Professional Interpreter level as is current practice.
- Interpreters should receive specific legal training on how to interpret for deaf people in different roles in court.
- That deaf jurors and interpreters be allowed time to brief and debrief at the beginning and end of each day during trial, in order to check for understanding, agreement of signs, etc.
- A predictive screening test for court interpreters of all languages be developed as per the United States Federal Court Interpreter Certification Examination (FCICE), which is enacted by The United States Court Interpreters Act (U.S. Congress, 1978), which requires that interpreters in U.S. federal courts be certified through a criterion-referenced performance test. The FCICE is a two-phase certification battery for federal court interpreters. Phase I is a multiple-choice Written Examination (WE) used to screen candidates for eligibility to take the Phase II criterion-referenced Oral Examination (OE), and thus filter out interpreters who do not have the adequate skills to interpret in court (Stansfield & Hewitt, 2005). This would be particularly important for Auslan/English interpreters working with deaf jurors.

This research can only be considered as a pilot due to the small number of participants. Nonetheless, this study has demonstrated that a small number of deaf people can understand excerpts from a judge's summation through English to Auslan interpretation, and that they are willing to participate in the judicial system as jurors. It does not, however, provide evidence for how deaf people can participate in, and make a significant contribution to, jury deliberations. Neither does it explore the potential impact of deaf jurors on the administration of justice from the perspective of the advocates, the bench, the accused, and witnesses.

Therefore further research is needed to investigate the deaf juror participation in court proceedings.

Impact of this Study

Based on the findings of this project, the NSW Law Reform Commission has recommended that deaf people be permitted to serve as jurors in NSW criminal courts. It is envisaged that the findings of this pilot study and the resulting recommendation will also influence considerations of Law Reform Commissions in other states in Australia, and will have national and international impact in demonstrating the extent to which deaf people can access courtroom proceedings and make a contribution to a jury.

Suggestions for Further Research

- Administration of the comprehension test on a larger scale throughout Australia, in order to collect data with statistical significance.
- Continuing on from Berk-Seligson's (1990), Hale's (2004), and Russell's (2002) research where they used mock trials to assess aspects of interpreting, conduct a mock trial over several days, filming the proceedings and jury deliberations and sentencing; and conduct interviews, comprehension tests, and discourse analyses of all participant utterances.
- Continuing on from Brennan and Brown's (1997) research in the United Kingdom, when deaf people are permitted to serve as jurors, carry out courtroom observations of real deaf juror experiences wherever possible.
- A collaborative study between the United States and Australia to compare comprehension and participation of jurors relying on signed and spoken language interpreters (i.e., Spanish, ASL, and Auslan).

REFERENCES

Angelelli, C. (2004). *Revisiting the interpreter's role: A study of conference, court, and medical interpreters in Canada, Mexico, and the United States.* Amsterdam: John Benjamins.

Banna, K. (2004). *Three court cases, nine professionals: What is the role of the court interpreter?* Paper presented at the Power to the Profession Conference, Melbourne, October 22–24.

Barber, J. (2005). Account of a deaf juror. *Sign Matters,* 25–32.

Barsky, R. (1996). The interpreter as intercultural agent in convention refugee hearings. *The Translator, 2* (1), 45–63.

Berk-Seligson, S. (1990). *The bilingual courtroom: Court interpreters in the judicial process.* Chicago: University of Chicago Press.

Berk-Seligson, S. (2002). The impact of politeness in witness testimony: The influence of the court interpreter. In F. Pöchhacker & M. Shlesinger (Eds.), *The interpreting studies reader* (pp. 278–292). London: Routledge.

Brennan, M. (1999). Signs of injustice. *The Translator, 5* (2), 221–246.

Brennan, M., & Brown, R. (2004). *Equality before the law: Deaf people's access to justice.* (2nd ed.). Coleford, UK: Douglas McLean.

Brindley, G., & Slatyer, H. (2002). Exploring task difficulty in ESL listening assessment. *Language Testing, 19* (4), 369–394.

Carroll, J. (1995). The use of interpreters in court. *Forensic Linguistics, 2* (1), 65–73.

Charrow, V. R., & Charrow, R. P. (1979a). Characteristics of the language of jury instruction. In J. E. Alatis & G. R. Tucker (Eds.), *Language in public life* (pp. 163–185). Washington, DC: Georgetown University Press.

Charrow, V. R., & Charrow, R. P. (1979b). Making legal language understandable: A psycholinguistic study of jury instructions. *Colombia Law Review, 79,* 1306–1374.

Colin, J., & Morris, R. (1996). *Interpreters and the legal process.* Winchester: Waterside Press.

Conley, J., & O'Barr, W. (1998). *Just words: Law, language and power.* Chicago: University of Chicago Press.

Cooke, M. (2002). Indigenous interpreting issue for courts. Australian Institute of Judicial Administration. Retrieved August 12, 2008, from http://www.aija.org.au/ac01/Cooke.pdf.

Cornes, A., Rohan, M., Napier, J., & Rey, J. (2006). Reading the signs: Impact of signed vs. written questionnaires on the prevalence of psychopathology among deaf adolescents. *Australia & New Zealand Journal of Psychiatry, 40* (8), 665–673.

Cotterill, J. (2000). Reading the rights: A cautionary tale of comprehension and comprehensibility. *Forensic Linguistics, 7* (1), 4–25.

Davis, J. (1990). *Interpreting in a language contact situation: The case of English-to-ASL interpretation.* Unpublished doctoral dissertation, University of New Mexico.

Davis, J. (2003). Cross-linguistic strategies used by interpreters. *Journal of Interpretation,* 95–128.

Deaf Blawg. (2006). Irish Deaf experience with jury duty. Retrieved December 19, 2006, from http://www.deaflawyers.org.uk/blawg/2004/08/irish_deaf_experience_with_jur.html.

Deaf man serves as juror. (2005, April 11). *Dominion Post.*

Dick, T. (2007, January 6–7). Nine angry jurors . . . and a few left confused. *The Sydney Morning Herald,* p. 16.

DPP. (2003). Jury selection. Retrieved October 20, 2003, from http://www.odpp.nsw.gov.au/guidelines/25%20Jury%20Selection.html.

Drew, P. (1990). Strategies in the contest between lawyer and witness in cross-examination. In J. Levi & A. Walker (Eds.), *Language in the judicial process* (pp. 39–64). New York: Plenum.

Dumas, B. K. (2000). US pattern jury instructions: Problems and proposals. *Forensic Linguistics, 7* (1), 49–71.

Eades, D. (2003). Participation of second language and second dialect speakers in the legal system. *Annual Review of Applied Linguistics, 23,* 113–133.

Edwards, A. B. (1995). *The practice of court interpreting.* Amsterdam: John Benjamins.

Ellman, F. (1992). Translator aids deaf juror in negligence trial. *New York Law Journal* (27 August).

Elwork, A., Sales, B. D., & Alfini, J. J. (1982). *Making jury instructions comprehensible.* Charlottesville, VA: Michie.

Enright, S. (1999). The Deaf juror and the thirteenth man. *New Law Journal* (1720).

Fenton, S. (1997). The role of the interpreter in the adversarial courtroom. In S. E. Carr, R. Roberts, A. Dufour, & D. Steyn (Eds.), *The Critical Link: Interpreters in the community* (pp. 29–34). Philadelphia: John Benjamins.

Fontana, S. (1999). Italian Sign Language and spoken Italian in contact: An analysis of interactions between Deaf parents and hearing children. In E. Winston (Ed.), *Storytelling and conversation: Discourse in Deaf communities* (pp. 149–161). Washington, DC: Gallaudet University Press.

Fournier, C. (1997). Courtroom interpretation for the Deaf in France. *Meta, 42* (3), 533–545.

Fowler, Y. (1997). The courtroom interpreter: Paragon and intruder? In S. E. Carr, R. Roberts, A. Dufour, & D. Steyn (Eds.), *The Critical Link: Interpreters in the community* (pp. 191–200). Philadelphia: John Benjamins.

Fowler, Y. (2003). Taking an interpreted witness statement at the police station: What did the witness actually say? In L. Brunette, G. Bastin, I. Hemlin & H. Clarke (Eds.), *The Critical Link 3: Interpreters in the community* (pp. 195–210). Philadelphia: John Benjamins.

Fryer-Smith, S. (2002). AIJA Aboriginal cultural awareness benchbook for western Australian courts (AIJA model indigenous benchbook project). Retrieved August 12, 2008, from http://www.aija.org.au/online/ICABenchbook.htm.

Gibbons, J. (1995). What got lost? The place of electronic recording and interpreters in police interviews. In D. Eades (Ed.), *Language in evidence: Issues confronting aboriginal and multicultural Australia* (pp. 175–186). Sydney: University of New South Wales Press.

Gibbons, J. (1999). Language and the law. *Annual Review of Applied Linguistics, 19*, 156–173.

Gibbons, J. (2003). *Forensic linguistics: An introduction to language in the justice system.* Oxford: Blackwell.

Golbas, M. (1981). Due process: The Deaf and blind as jurors. *New England Law Review, 17,* 119.

Goldflam, R. (1995). Silence in court! Problems and prospects in Aboriginal legal interpreting. In D. Eades (Ed.), *Language in evidence: Issues confronting aboriginal and multicultural Australia* (pp. 28–54). Sydney: University of New South Wales Press.

Gonzalez, R. D., Vasquez, V. F., & Mikkelson, H. (1992). *Fundamentals of court interpretation: Theory, policy, and practice.* Tucson: Institute for Court Interpretation, University of Arizona.

Graessar, A., Mills, K., & Zwaan, R. (1997). Discourse comprehension. *Annual Review of Psychology, 48,* 163–189.

Hale, S. (1996). Pragmatic considerations in court interpreting. *Australian Review of Applied Linguistics, 19* (1), 61–72.

Hale, S. (1997a). Clash of world perspectives: The discursive practices of the law, the witness and the interpreter. *Forensic Linguistics, 4* (2), 197–209.

Hale, S. (1997b). The interpreter on trial. Pragmatics in court interpreting. In S. E. Carr, R. Roberts, A. Dufour, & D. Steyn (Eds.), *The Critical Link: Interpreters in the community* (pp. 201–211). Philadelphia: John Benjamins.

Hale, S. (1997c). The treatment of register variation in court interpreting. *The Translator, 3* (1), 39–54.

Hale, S. (1999). The interpreter's treatment of discourse markers in courtroom questions. *Forensic Linguistics, 6* (1), 57–82.

Hale, S. (2001). How are courtroom questions interpreted? An analysis of Spanish interpreters' practices. In I. Mason (Ed.), *Triadic exchanges: Studies in dialogue interpreting* (pp. 21–50). Manchester, UK: St. Jerome.

Hale, S. (2002). How faithfully do court interpreters render the style of non-English speaking witnesses's testimonies? A data based study of Spanish-English bilingual proceedings. *Discourse Studies, 4* (1), 25–48.

Hale, S., & Gibbons, J. (1999). Varying realities: Patterned changes in the interpreter's representation of courtroom and external realities. *Applied Linguistics, 20* (1), 203–220.

Hale, S. (2004). *The discourse of court interpreting: Discourse practices of the law, the witness and the interpreter.* Philadelphia: John Benjamins.

Hambleton, R., & De Jong, J. (2003). Advances in translating and adapting educational and psychological tests. *Language Testing, 20* (2), 127–134.

Hambleton, R., & Patsula, L. (1999). Increasing the validity of adapted tests: Myths to be avoided and guidelines for improving test adaptation practices. *Journal of Applied Testing Technology, 1*(1), 1–30.

Hansen, S., Dirksen, R., Kuchler, M., Kunz, K., & Neumann, S. (2006). Comprehensible legal texts: Utopia or a question of wording? On processing rephrased German court decisions. *Hermes, 36*, 15–40.

Howard, D., Quinn, S., Blokland, J., & Flynn, M. (1993). Aboriginal hearing loss and the criminal justice system. Retrieved August 12, 2008, from http://www.austlii.edu.au/au/journals/AboriginalLB/1993/58.html.

Hughes, A. (1989). *Testing for language teachers.* Cambridge: Cambridge University Press.

Johnston, T. (2002). The representation of English using Auslan: Implications for Deaf bilingualism and English literacy. *Australian Journal of Education of the Deaf, 8*, 23–37.

Johnston, T., & Schembri, A. (2007). *Australian Sign Language (Auslan): An introduction to sign linguistics.* Cambridge: Cambridge University Press.

Kadric, M. (2000). Interpreting in the Austrian courtroom. In R. Roberts, S. E. Carr, D. Abraham, & A. Dufour (Eds.), *The Critical Link 2: Interpreters in the community* (pp. 153–165). Philadelphia: John Benjamins.

Kelly, A. M. (2000). Cultural parameters for interpreters in the courtroom. In R. Roberts, S. E. Carr, D. Abraham, & A. Dufour (Eds.), *The Critical Link 2: Interpreters in the community* (pp. 131–152). Philadelphia: John Benjamins.

Krouglov, A. (1999). Police interpreting: Politeness and sociocultural context. *The Translator, 5* (2), 285–302.

Kurlander, K. (2008). Walking the fine line. In P. Hauser, K. Finch, & A. Hauser (Eds.), *Deaf professionals and designated interpreters working together: A new paradigm.* Washington, DC: Gallaudet University Press.

Lane, C., McKenzie-Bridle, K., & Curtis, L. (1999). The right to interpreting and translation services in New Zealand courts. *Forensic Linguistics, 6* (1), 115–136.

Levi, J. N. (1993). Evaluating jury comprehension of Illinois capital-sentencing instructions. *American Speech, 68* (1), 20–49.

Language Services Section, NJ Administrative Office of the Courts. (2000). *Guidelines for trials involving deaf jurors who serve with the assistance of sign language interpreters.* Retrieved August 12, 2008, from http://www.judiciary.state.nj.us/interpreters/wrkgdeafjur.pdf.

Lucas, C., & Valli, C. (1992). *Language contact in the American deaf community.* San Diego: Academic Press.

Luginbuhl, J. (1992). Comprehension of a judge's instructions in the penalty phase of a capital trial. *Law & Human Behaviour, 16*, 203–218.

Maley, Y., Candlin, C. N., Koster, P., & Crichton, J. (1995). Orientations in lawyer-client interviews. *Forensic Linguistics, 2* (1), 42–55.

Mather, S., & Mather, R. (2003). Court interpreting for signing jurors: Just transmitting or interpreting? In C. Lucas (Ed.), *Language and the law in deaf communities* (pp. 60–81). Washington, DC: Gallaudet University Press.

Mathers, C. (2006). *Sign language interpreters in court: Understanding best practice*. Bloomington, IN: Authorhouse.

McCay, V., & Miller, K. (2001). Linguistic incompetence to stand trial: A unique condition in some deaf defendants. *Journal of Interpretation*, 99–120.

McCay, V., & Miller, K. (2005). Obstacles faced by deaf people in the criminal justice system. *American Annals of the Deaf, 150* (3), 283–291.

McNamara, T. (2000). *Language testing*. Oxford: Oxford University Press.

Mikkelson, H. (1998). Towards a redefinition of the role of the court interpreter. *Interpreting, 3* (1), 21–46.

Mikkelson, H. (2000). *Introduction to court interpreting*. Manchester, UK: St Jerome Publishing.

Miller, K. (2001). Access to sign language interpreters in the criminal justice system. *American Annals of the Deaf, 146* (4), 328–330.

Miller, K. (2003). Signs of prison life: Linguistic adaptations of deaf inmates. *Journal of Interpretation*, 129–142.

Miller, K., & McCay, V. (1994). Qualifications of sign language interpreters in the criminal justice system. *Journal of Interpretation*, 111–124.

Miller, K. R., & McCay, V. (2001). Linguistic diversity in deaf defendants and due process rights. *Journal of Deaf Studies and Deaf Education, 6* (3), 226–234.

Montalvo, M. B. (2001). *Interpreting for non-English speaking jurors: Analysis of a new and complex responsibility*. Paper presented at the American Translators' Association annual meeting, October 31–November 3, Los Angeles, CA.

Montoya, L. A., Egnatovitch, R., Eckhardt, E., Goldstein, M., Goldstein, R. A., & Steinberg, A. (2004). Translation challenges and strategies: The ASL translation of a computer-based psychiatric diagnostic interview. *Sign Language Studies, 4* (4), 314–344.

Morris, R. (1999). The face of justice: Historical aspects of court interpreting. *Interpreting, 4* (1), 97–124.

Napier, J. (2002). University interpreting: Linguistic issues for consideration. *Journal of Deaf Studies and Deaf Education, 7* (4), 281–301.

Napier, J. (2006). Comparing language contact phenomena between Auslan/English interpreters and deaf Australians: A preliminary study. In C. Lucas (Ed.), *From the Great Plains to Australia: Multilingualism and sign languages* (pp. 39–78). Washington DC: Gallaudet University Press.

Napier, J., & Rohan, M. (2007). An invitation to dance: Deaf consumers' perceptions of signed language interpreters and interpreting. In M. Metzger & E. Fleetwood (Eds.), *Translation, sociolinguistic, and consumer issues in interpreting* (Vol. 3, pp. 159–203). Washington, DC: Gallaudet University Press.

Nardi, M. (2005). Vulnerable groups—Deaf people at official hearings: A perspective of the European Forum of Sign Language Interpreters. In H. Keijzer-Lambooy & W. J. Gasille (Eds.), *Aequilibrium: Instruments for lifting language barriers in intercultural legal proceedings* (pp. 69–76). Utrecht: ITV Hogeschool voor Tolken en Vertalen.

NEON. (2006). The jury's in [Electronic Version]. Retrieved December 19, 2006, from http://www.neon.org.nz/newsarchive/thejuryisin/.

NSWLRC. (2004). *Blind or deaf jurors* (Discussion paper 46). Sydney: New South Wales Law Reform Commission.

Olsson, J. (2004). *Forensic linguistics: An introduction to language, crime and the law*. London: Continuum.

Pöllabauer, S. (2004). Interpreting in asylum hearings. *Interpreting, 6* (2), 143–180.

Robinson, L. (1994). *Handbook for legal interpreters*. Sydney: Law Book Company.

Russell, D. (2002). *Interpreting in legal contexts: Consecutive and simultaneous interpretation*. Burtonsville, MD: Sign Media.

Schweda Nicholson, N. (1994). Professional ethics for court and community interpreters. In D. L. Hammond (Ed.), *Professional issues for translators and interpreters* (Vol. 7, pp. 79–98). Amsterdam: John Benjamins.

Shuy, R. (1998). *The language of confession, interrogation and deception*. Thousand Oaks, CA: Sage.

Shuy, R. (2001). Discourse analysis in the legal context. In D. Schiffrin, D. Tannen, & H. E. Hamilton (Eds.), *The handbook of discourse analysis* (pp. 437–452). Oxford: Blackwell.

Shuy, R. (2003). The language problems of minorities in the legal setting. In C. Lucas (Ed.), *Language and the law in Deaf communities* (pp. 1–20). Washington, DC: Gallaudet University Press.

Silas, D. (1993). Deaf jurors. *New Law Journal* (18 June), 896.

Stansfield, C. (2003). Test translation and adaptation in public education in the USA. *Language Testing, 20* (2), 189–207.

Stansfield, C., & Hewitt, W. (2005). Examining the predictive validity of a screening test for court interpreters. *Language Testing, 22* (4), 438–462.

Steele, W. W., & Thornburg, E. G. (1988). Jury instructions: A persistent failure to communicate. *North Carolina Law Review, 67*, 77–119.

Stevens, H. (2005). Justice must be seen to be done. In H. Keijzer-Lambooy & W. J. Gasille (Eds.), *Aequilibrium: Instruments for lifting language barriers in intercultural legal proceedings* (pp. 77–86). Utrecht: ITV Hogeschool voor Tolken en Vertalen.

Tiersma, P. (1999). *Legal language*. Chicago: University of Chicago Press.

Tilbury, N. (2005). Specific attention for vulnerable groups—In particular those with hearing impairments and sign language users—Legislation, practical issues and training. In H. Keijzer-Lambooy & W. J. Gasille (Eds.), *Aequilibrium: Instruments for lifting language barriers in intercultural legal proceedings* (pp. 61–68). Utrecht: ITV Hogeschool voor Tolken en Vertalen.

Travaglia, S. (2005). Deaf person to serve on jury. *Resource: The official newsletter of the Disability Resource Centre Auckland*, 5.

Turner, G. H. (1995). The bilingual, bimodal courtroom: A first glance. *Journal of Interpretation, 7* (1), 3–34.

Turner, G. H., & Brown, R. (2001). Interaction and the role of the interpreter in court. In F. J. Harrington & G. H. Turner (Eds.), *Interpreting interpreting: Studies and reflections on sign language interpreting* (pp. 152–167). Coleford, UK: Douglas McLean.

Wilcox, P. (1995). Dual interpretation and discourse effectiveness in legal settings. *Journal of Interpretation, 7* (1), 89–98.

Zambrano, M. (2006). *The interpreter's linguistic power: A new courtroom reality in immigration hearings*. University of Pittsburgh.

Interpreter Preparation Conversations:

Multiple Perspectives

Debra Russell

In recent years there has been a trend to employ teams of signed language interpreters in a number of contexts in order to best address the needs of the interpreting assignment. There have been a number of factors identified that necessitate the need for teams of interpreters. The rationale utilized for employing a team is often based on the complexity of the work, the importance of providing the most accurate work by reducing the cognitive and mental fatigue that can occur in assignments where only one interpreter is working, and the length of the assignment. In many North American contexts, these factors have shaped hiring practices and interpreter education practices. A pressing reason to employ teams of interpreters has been to reduce the number of repetitive-motion injuries, and to reduce the fatigue experienced by interpreters (Demers, 2005). In addition, there are prevailing notions that the use of two or more interpreters may improve the accuracy of the interpretation, enhance the psychological support the interpreters provide for one another, and contribute to the professional development of the interpreters (Frishberg, 1986; Solow, 2000). Stewart, Schein, and Cartwright (2005) cite an interview with an interpreter educator in which accuracy is cited as a primary reason to use teams. The expectation is that team interpreters will correct incorrect signed and spoken interpretations and support the actively working interpreter by filling in unheard or miscued speech.

Frishberg (1986) identified several circumstances requiring the use of teams of interpreters, including the spatial arrangements of the room or number of participants, the length of the assignment, and the varieties of language or communications systems used in an interaction. Both Shaw (2003) and Cokely (2003) have explored the nature of interpreters working in teams. Shaw examined how interpreters who have been hired to monitor the work of other interpreters working in legal settings function as part of a legal team, serving both courts and defense attorneys. Her findings reveal that the linguistic and cultural skills of the monitoring interpreters must be of an exceptional quality in order to be able to discern what interpreting errors must be brought to the attention of the courts. Her work also reveals the ways in which monitoring interpreters' interactions with teams of interpreters can affect the quality of the overall work presented in a courtroom. When major errors in the interpretation have been brought to the attention of the court, there are numerous benefits, from saving the court time in costly retrials to allowing proceedings to continue after the corrections are made in a way that is efficient and supports the judicial process. Cokely reported significant discrepancies between the behaviors interpreters identified they would use to ask for support and the actual behaviors that they used to request support. His study showed interpreters in preliminary meetings mentioned 7 behaviors that they would use to ask for support, but during the actual interpretation there were 16 different behaviors that were used by them to request support.

The two national professional organizations representing signed language interpreters in North America, the Registry of Interpreters for the Deaf (RID) and the Association of Visual Language Interpreters of Canada (AVLIC), have both cited the need for effective interpreting in teams in their Codes of Ethics and Guidelines for Professional Conduct. Both Codes of Ethics explicitly note the need to demonstrate professional accountability for one's work, and to collaborate with team members in a manner that reflects professional standards during all phases of assignments (AVLIC, 2000; RID, 2005). More recently, Witter-Merithew and Johnson (2005) undertook a research project to identify the competencies needed by interpreters in order to address the gap between interpreter education and readiness to work. The authors cite wide-spread agreement among educators, consumers, and interpreter practitioners about the various skill sets required by practitioners that allow for self and peer analysis of interpreting performance, and the human relations and professionalism competencies that underlie team performance.

Despite these beliefs and agreed upon work practices that support the use of teams, some research has shown that an interpreting team does not always monitor the interaction, communicate well within the team, or provide effective support (Russell, 2002, 2005). In that study, a significant number of interpreting errors were not consistently corrected by teams of interpreters, leaving the court unknowingly with interpreting errors on the record. The study also revealed interaction patterns between team members that affected the success of the team experience.

The study demonstrated how these interaction patterns among interpreters affected the Deaf witness, who in turn lost trust in the team. Clearly the goal is for conscientious and competent interpreting teams that can ensure that the interpretation is effective and accurate. It seems that such a goal is not always achieved for a number of possible reasons, including a lack of interpreter education and interpreting experience, a lack of assignment preparation by interpreters working as a team, and an inability to adequately manage the interpreting process as a team. This chapter attempts to further our understanding of the nature of the work of interpreters functioning in teams by exploring the data that were collected as part of a larger study. That data examined the ways in which interpreters prepare to work together and prepare consumers to work with them. The perceptions of multiple perspectives on team interpreting, from the lens of interpreters, Deaf witnesses, and non-deaf expert witness, lawyers and judges will be highlighted.

THE STUDY—OBJECTIVES, METHOD, AND PARTICIPANTS

One of the research objectives of the study conducted in 2000 was to investigate the preparation strategies of interpreters when working together as a team, including the specific ways in which the interpreters prepare with each other prior to beginning the interpretation, and how they prepared the lawyers and Deaf witnesses to work with interpreters. This research objective was embedded within a larger study of consecutive and simultaneous interpreting use in criminal trials (Russell, 2002, 2005). The mock trials were based on real court cases and involved the use of lawyers and judges, Deaf witnesses, and a non-deaf expert witness. The trials were taped in a moot courtroom within a law school. The discourse was not scripted, and the interpretation was videotaped in order to allow for complete discourse analysis of the work at the conclusion of the trials. Further analysis of the data as it relates to preparation strategies has been conducted for this chapter.

Prior to interpreting the trials, interpreters were assigned to teams of two per each 90 minute trial, and each interpreter worked two trials with a different interpreter on each occasion. The preparation conversations held by interpreters were then tape recorded for later analysis. In addition, the interpreters were recorded when speaking with the lawyers, expert witness, and Deaf witnesses prior to the trials. At the completion of the trials, the researcher interviewed the interpreters about their work and team processes. The interviews were semi-structured and the interpreters were invited to reflect on their experiences, guided by several general questions that probed their impressions of their work, including their preparation strategies, reflections on what had worked well in the interpreting and what had not been as successful, and what they would do differently in the future. Finally, interviews were held with the expert witness, the lawyers, and the judges about their perceptions of the interpretation and the processes they observed as consumers of the interpreting service.

The four Canadian interpreters who participated in this study included three females and one male. Three interpreters held national AVLIC certification at the time, and one did not hold certification; however, the interpreter was selected based on the experience s/he had in legal interpreting. All of the interpreters possessed a minimum of 5 years interpreting experience in legal settings, had a minimum of 15 years experience using American Sign Language (ASL) and interpreting in non-legal settings, and three of the interpreters had significant experience and training in legal settings (1000–3000 hours). Of the four interpreters, one had Deaf parents. None of the interpreters had worked with each other prior to these trials, which necessitated the need for explicit conversations about how the team processes would be implemented. All of the interpreters reported regularly working in team contexts in legal and other settings.

Two female Deaf persons participated in the study as Deaf witnesses. Both attended a school for the Deaf, used ASL as their preferred language, and had experience using professional interpreters. Nine lawyers participated in this study and each had practiced criminal law for a minimum of three years and had at least 150 hours of actual courtroom experience. Four of the lawyers had limited experience working with either a signed or spoken language interpreter, and three of the lawyers had been exposed to some professional development during their legal training about working with interpreters and Deaf community members. Finally, there were three judges who were part of this study. One had extensive experience working with spoken language interpreters using aboriginal languages, the second judge had never seen a signed language interpreter before this experience, and the third judge had limited experience with both spoken and signed language interpreters.

DATA ANALYSIS AND FINDINGS

The data were coded and analyzed for the themes that emerged, using descriptive and pattern codes based on qualitative analysis methods (Miles & Huberman, 1994). The following themes emerged from the interpreters' preparation conversations, and from the interviews with all participants.

Interpreter Preparation Conversations

Prior to interpreting the trials, the interpreters were given 45 minutes to prepare with each other, and then had additional time to prepare with the witnesses and the lawyers. The conversations held between the interpreters demonstrated that these four interpreters had a series of questions or a framework that was commonly used to begin their collegial conversations. The questions concerned these topics

- Sharing the work—The interpreters addressed how to manage the interpreting process, with one team choosing to split the work by language considerations. In that situation, it was determined that one interpreter would perform the ASL to English interpretation during the Deaf witness testimony, and the second interpreter would perform the English to ASL interpretation. The three other teams chose to split the work based on time periods of 20 minute blocks, where one interpreter would assume the active interpreting position for 20 minutes and the second interpreter would offer support by monitoring the work and correcting errors when needed.
- Interpretation Accuracy—The interpreters identified strategies that would support meaningful and effective interpretation while facilitating the interaction. For example, they spoke of how they would monitor each other's work and offer information to correct or supplement an original interpretation. These strategies involved taking notes to support the interpretation, providing visual and auditory feedback to the interpreter about their work, stopping speakers or signers for clarification, as well as the use of signals to stop speakers/signers in order to manage the interpreting process.

- Strategies to Support Each Other—The interpreters identified behaviors that would be required and requested by the active interpreter when s/he needed the support of the monitoring interpreter. As in the Cokely (2003) study, these included: leaning towards the interpreting partner, indicating what they needed, eye gaze, and tapping each other. While two of the four interpreters discussed the role of notes in consecutive interpreting, there was no mention of whether the notes would be used as a communication vehicle between the two interpreters when requesting or offering support to each other.
- Signals—The interpreters discussed the signals that they would use to provide each other with information to correct or adjust interpretations and the signals that they would use to ask participants in the interpreted event to pause or repeat a message. Two of the four teams reached an agreement that before stopping a participant, the active interpreter would seek support through an interpreter feed. These teams indicated that an interpreter feed was seen as the provision of information by the other interpreter who was not in the active interpreting role. The information could be an omitted word or phrase, a word or phrase that corrects an inaccurate interpretation, or could involve the other interpreter taking over the active role if the feed required was lengthy and was going to disrupt the process. Most teams indicated a preference for information to be signed in ASL by their interpreting partner, if the interpretation was from English to ASL, as in the case of working with the non-deaf expert witness. When the interpreting involved the Deaf witnesses, the teams indicated they preferred to be supported by spoken English feeds as the interpreters were standing next to each other to provide the interpretation. Position appeared to drive the choice of information being offered in spoken English or in ASL (standing beside each other, or facing each other). Also, two interpreters identified areas of interpreting weakness that they wanted the monitoring interpreter to attend to, and presumably have the interpreter feed the correct information, for example, "I will probably miss the fingerspelling" or "Just tell me if I have the tense wrong." Finally, it should be noted that none of the interpreters in their preparation conversations addressed the volume of the feed in spoken English, which again

is similar to the Cokely (2003) study. It may be that the interpreters understood that the feed in spoken English was to be whispered; however this was never explicitly stated.

- Preparing the Lawyers—The interpreters addressed how they would prepare the lawyers for the needs of the interpreters in the legal settings and how they would deal with the legal discourse. All the interpreting teams had prior basic information about the legal case (nature of the charges, names of witnesses, time frame for the alleged offense) and they identified questions that they would like to ask the lawyers. They also identified aspects that they would like to share with the Court that could ensure the interpreting went well.
- Shared Meaning, Contexts, and Experiences—Three out of four of the teams of interpreters spent approximately ten minutes of their time together exchanging information about how much experience each team member had in similar work settings. They posed questions to each other about their interpreting experience, especially in legal contexts, and tried to ascertain if they had common experiences from which to build upon for this assignment. The interpreters also spoke of their past experience with team interpreting, articulating their understanding of what it means to be a team player. For example, does it mean Interpreter A does twenty minutes of work, and is replaced by Interpreter B, with very little support or monitoring from the non-active interpreter, or does it mean that each share the responsibility for the success or the lack of success of the mediated communication event?
- Views of Interpreting Models—One of the interpreting teams also addressed how they conceptualized interpreting. For this team, both members identified how they viewed interpretation, especially during the Deaf witness testimony, as a communication event that involved interpreting as mediated communication, based on the constructed dialogue of the lawyers and the witnesses. As Pöchhacker (2004) describes, this meme of interpreting brings together language, cognition, interaction, and culture as a reference for interpreting. None of the other teams attempted to discuss their conceptual frames of reference for interpreting despite the fact such frames can impact on the nature of the team process. For example, if one team member views

interpreting as linguistic transfer void of cultural overlays and the other interpreter views the work as linguistic and cultural mediation, the Deaf witness is going to see two very different styles of interpreting within the interaction. This is what occurred in one trial and it is discussed in the Deaf Witness Interview section of this chapter.

- Spokesperson—One of the interpreting teams determined that only one of them would approach the lawyers to conduct the preparation conversation, taking on the spokesperson role. The other three teams chose to hold the conversations as a team.

Preparation Conversations with Non-Deaf Lawyers

All teams took the time to hold preparation conversations with the lawyers, and while there was consistency among the kinds of questions and comments made, there were also key differences demonstrated by one of the teams. For the team that had chosen a spokesperson, both interpreters were present for the meeting, and the spokesperson took the lead on the conversation. On two occasions the other interpreter offered additional clarification and responded to the lawyer's questions. All of the teams described the interpreting process between two languages, providing information laden with interpreter technical terms such as *the interpreting process, consecutive and simultaneous interpreting,* and *miscues.* The interpreters also took the time to discuss the signals that would be used to pause the lawyers, and these ranged from "I will look at you," "I will ask you to pause" to "I will hold up one finger." The interpreters also addressed how they would behave as a team and that there would be occasions when the interpreters needed to confer with each other about the accuracy of the interpretation.

During these preparation conversations, the interpreters did not ask questions about the content of the case or key documents that might be useful for them to view prior to beginning the trials. Nor did any of the teams ask the lawyers if they had questions for the interpreters. It is interesting to note that interpreters working in legal settings often report that they request and utilize materials in order to prepare for the work, and yet that did not occur here. While the mock trial context may have contributed to this factor, it may also be that what interpreters report doing and what they actually do in the area of preparation is different. It may also be a function of the amount of time the interpreters spent with the lawyers, and if so, this speaks to the need to prioritize discussion items when there is a limited time so that all the key areas have been addressed.

Preparation Conversations with Deaf Witnesses

The interpreters also had an opportunity to meet with the Deaf witness prior to each trial. What emerged from those preparation conversations was agreement across all four teams that it was important that each team member have an opportunity to converse in ASL with the Deaf witness, in order to determine the witness's language style and preferences and to create a rapport that would facilitate effective interpretation. The interpreters also acknowledged that it was important for the Deaf witness to see their use of ASL in order for the Deaf witness to begin to trust the capabilities of the interpreters. The interpreters and the Deaf witnesses engaged in conversations that revealed information about the Deaf person's early school experiences, involvement in the Deaf community, and the nature of language in use as it applied to the consumer's use of ASL.

These conversations support the notion that in the case of interpreted interactions, the interpreters and the receiver are "co-participants in the co-construction of meaning" (Wadjensjö, 1998). The interpreters seemed to demonstrate an intuitive sensitivity that they could not just interpret in the courtroom without having some sense of the Deaf consumer's past experience and language use, as this would support the interpreter in the re-creation of the Deaf person's narrative within the courtroom context.

Only one team specifically addressed how they viewed interpreting as interaction in their preparation conversation, but all of the teams through their actions demonstrated an awareness of the concept of meaning as articulated by Wilcox and Shaffer (2005). Wilcox and Shaffer suggest that meaning is not something objective to be found in the words and constructions of language, but rather it is co-constructed between participants in an immediate social context. The interpreters demonstrated this concept by conversing in ASL about topics that would help the interpreters understand how the Deaf person may construct their specific narrative for this specific situation, knowing that the narrative would unfold through the questions asked by lawyers. The interpreters did not probe for details specific to the case, but rather, spent the time focusing on exchanging information between themselves and the Deaf person. For example, the interpreters also shared their personal language journey narrative about how they came to interpreting, where they learned ASL, and the nature of their Deaf community interaction in the city in which they reside. Unlike the preparation conversations with lawyers, here the interpreters did not explicitly describe how they would work in the court. It may be that the interpreters assumed that the Deaf consumers had a great deal of experience using interpreters and this was not needed. However neither Deaf person in these mock situations had experience with interpreters in courtroom settings, adding to the reality of the simulation.

Preparation Conversation with Expert Witness

Each trial included expert witness testimony and the expert witness made themselves available to the interpreters for a brief conversation prior to the trial. Three out of the four interpreting teams chose to engage in conversation with the witness. What emerged from the preparation conversations was an emphasis by the interpreters on their needs to the exclusion of the needs of the witness. The interpreters stressed that they would be taking turns interpreting the testimony, how they would stop the witness during consecutive interpreting, the process they would use to correct errors and what they needed to do in order to provide successful interpretation. One team addressed the area of witness goals within their testimony. However, the other teams did not ask the witness about the nature and scope of their testimony and areas that the witness would likely highlight. All of the interpreting teams requested a summation of the witness's qualifications based on the person's résumé. None of the teams explored whether the expert witness had questions or concerns about working with interpreters.

Deaf Witness Interview Results

The Deaf witnesses commented on the trials from the perspective of being able to share their narrative and how effective the interpreting had to be in order for them to feel like they had meaningful access to the judicial procedures. It was interesting to note that the Deaf witnesses expressed the most comfort with the interpreter with the least amount of courtroom experience. They reported that the interpreter appeared to be a fluent and natural language user, and was confident when presenting the interpretation. There was strong agreement between the witnesses that this interpreter was also able to consistently present the work in ASL with near native-like fluency. The witnesses acknowledge that all of the interpreters were fluent in ASL. There were times however that the interpretation reverted to more English-like work, which was less comprehensible to the witnesses. The native-like fluency in ASL created a sense of comfort and trust for the witness. The witnesses noted that this interpreter also demonstrated sensitivity to the Deaf witnesses' emotional states when preparing for the trials by not asking specific case details, but rather engaging in conversation. Through this conversation, the Deaf witnesses felt confident that the interpreter would understand their messages and be able to represent their voices and experiences in the courtroom.

There were several themes that emerged across the interviews with Deaf witnesses, as it related to the team interpreting process. The themes included

- <u>Conferring: Purpose and Effect on Witness</u>—Deaf consumers reported being distracted by the interpreters who appeared to be over-conferring with their team member. Each time the interpreters would visibly pause and confer with each other, the Deaf consumer questioned how well they understood the witness's use of ASL. While the witnesses acknowledged that they would like the interpreters to stop them if the interpreters were not sure, they also said that when it occurred several times they began to lose faith in the abilities of the interpreters.
- <u>Error Correction</u>—Deaf witnesses questioned how clear it was to the judge and the lawyers when the interpreters corrected themselves; as Deaf witnesses they could not hear what the interpreters said and hence wondered what strategies the interpreters used to make it explicit that it was an interpreting error versus the witness changing an answer. One Deaf witness reported that s/he appreciated when the team addressed errors by one interpreter signing contemporaneously what the other interpreter spoke to the court about the error and the correction needed. This strategy was only used by one of the four teams.
- <u>Interpreter Behavior: Nervousness and Team Processes</u>—This theme was raised often in the interviews conducted with the Deaf witnesses after the trials. The witnesses indicated that

when the interpreter demonstrated nervousness, as visible on his/her face and hands, it influenced the witnesses who then tried to change their linguistic use of ASL to ensure the interpreter could understand them. Further, the Deaf witnesses commented that when the interpreters had very different linguistic styles, for example, when one interpreter had a native style of ASL and the other interpreter had less native-like use of ASL, it was challenging for the Deaf witnesses to adapt to the style differences after the interpreters switched. One witness described it as watching a tennis match, where your brain has to switch back and forth watching the two different players. A significant incident in one trial led a witness to comment that how the teams functioned together in the courtroom had a dramatic impact on his/her courtroom testimony. During the trial, the two interpreters were to have exchanged places, relieving each other during the English to ASL expert witness testimony. When Interpreter A indicated it was time to switch, Interpreter B responded in ASL indicating that s/he was fine and would continue to interpret. Despite three attempts by Interpreter A to relieve Interpreter B, no switch took place, leaving the first interpreter to work an hour in duration. The Deaf witness could see the interaction but other members of the court who do not use ASL had no awareness of the situation. This decision not to switch resulted in an increase in interpreting miscues, and perhaps more importantly, left the Deaf witness with a negative impression of this team's ability to share the work professionally.

- Notetaking: Purpose and Disposal of Notes—Deaf witnesses reported that they noticed some interpreting teams taking notes during the use of consecutive interpreting, however no mention was made pre- or post-trial to the witness about what the notes were to contain and how they would be used. Deaf witnesses reported that they would have preferred the interpreting teams explain this in the pre-conference meeting, so that all had a shared understanding of the purpose of the notetaking, and most importantly, how the notes would be disposed of after the trial.
- Preferences: Confident Interpreter—The Deaf witnesses in this study reported that they were most comfortable working with the interpreter who appeared the most confident and had the most natural language use in ASL. Ironically, this turned out to

be the interpreter with the least amount of legal interpreting training and experience. This interpreter has Deaf parents and over 15 years of interpreting experience in a variety of non-legal settings.

JUDGES AND LAWYER INTERVIEW RESULTS

All of the lawyers in this study indicated that they appreciated the preparation conversations and seven of the nine lawyers commented that they had never experienced this approach with spoken language interpreters in similar trials.

"I was surprised when they told us what they were doing. I have never worked with a signer before but the spoken language interpreters never tell us what they are doing! I appreciated this approach."

While the lawyers indicated they appreciated this opportunity, they also reported feeling overwhelmed by the content of the conversation. For example, the lawyers expressed that the interpreters described what it was they would be doing, using terms that were unfamiliar to the lawyers (e.g. interpreter miscues, consecutive and simultaneous interpreting, support, and active interpreter, etc.), and the interpreters seemed to be "controlling" at times. The lawyers also said that they would have appreciated the use of examples when describing the nature of interpreting.

The lawyers viewed the interpreters as professional and appropriate for the setting, but they would have preferred the conversation to be more like a dialogue versus a monologue. In terms of a dialogue, the lawyers expressed surprise that the interpreters did not ask trial specific questions in order to establish a complete frame of reference. As with the Deaf witnesses in this study, the judges and the lawyers had considerable questions about the manner and the frequency in which interpreters were conferring with each other. The judges noted that they thought the interpreters appeared professional in their interactions with the lawyers and the witnesses, but they did not understand why the interpreters were "checking" with each other. The lawyers recalled that they had been told how the team would function prior to the trial, but they had not understood that this conferring behavior was related to error correction and they were not prepared for the frequency that this would occur. One lawyer stated, "I started to wonder if they knew what they were doing. I felt concerned about how often it occurred and I didn't understand why they were doing this."

Error correction was a critical element that the lawyers reported that they had hoped the interpreters would address in the preparation conversations but they did not feel this was handled effectively. Some of the lawyers also felt the conferring interfered with their line of questioning, as they were distracted by it and the frequent pauses altered the lawyer's "flow of questions." The judges commented on the fact that they would have preferred the Crown prosecutors to review some of these basic interpreting behaviors with them prior to the trial. While the judges understood the need for conferring, they also recommended that the interpreters always seek permission prior to conferring, and to indicate why they are conferring with each other. If the conferring takes more than a few seconds the judges would rather that the question/answer be repeated, and that they will direct that interaction, not the interpreters.

Neither the judges nor the lawyers understood why the interpreters were displaying attending behaviors such as nodding affirmatively at the Deaf witness during testimony. The interpreters reported this behavior was a form of backchannel feedback to the witness to indicate that the interpreters understood them, and this is an appropriate convention in signed language use. The lawyers and the judges viewed the behavior as "encouraging the deaf witness." Again, this was not addressed in the preparation conversations, and given the lawyers and the judges differing levels of experience with minority language forms, let alone ASL, it would have been helpful information.

One judge and several lawyers expressed a preference for one team member over another when performing the ASL to English work, indicating that they preferred the interpreter who made clear statements of error correction, for example: "Interpreter correction—that was 12 people not 10," and the interpreter who appeared to be able to convey the emotional affect of the witness. None of the lawyers and the judges was comfortable with the interpreters' use of the phrase "interpreter miscue" to describe an error. All of the lawyers expressed surprise at how effectively the interpreters were able to convey the emotions of the Deaf witness. They had anticipated this would be an area of weakness, and suggested that this specific topic would have been helpful to canvas in the preparation conversation.

Unlike the Deaf witnesses, the judges and the lawyers had no awareness of the team that experienced the difficulty over exchanging active interpreting positions, and when made aware of it during the interview, they expressed a view indicating such behavior was inappropriate during an interpreted court interaction, and that when these interpreter- to-interpreter messages are not available to the court it creates issues for them.

Finally, the lawyers and the judges reported that positioning of the interpreters was not something addressed in the preparation conversations, and yet was one of the elements that were problematic. For example, the lawyers reported being surprised that the interpreters would need to have their backs to the lawyers in order to face the Deaf witness, and at one point in a trial, the judge requested the interpreter change positions so the judge could see them more clearly, which changed the sight lines for the Deaf witness. This situation took several minutes to resolve in order to ensure the judge understood why the interpreters had to be positioned as they were in order for the Deaf person to be able to see the interpreter and have access to the testimony of the witness. This problem could have been avoided if the Crown prosecutor had a clearer understanding of what the courtroom positioning requirements were and then s/he could have oriented the judge prior to the trial.

Expert Witness Results

The expert witness post-trial interview revealed several issues. The witness was interested in why the one team chose not to have any conversation prior to the trial, and this left the expert witness with a reduced trust level for the interpreting work of this team. The expert witness also suggested that the team that asked about the goals or nature of the testimony inspired confidence, leading the witness to believe that their interpreting work would be stronger. The witness noted that all of the interpreters who engaged in preparation conversations asked about academic and professional qualifications that provided them with a frame for the qualifying part of the court accepting the witness during the trial. However, the witness had a briefing article prepared for the court that identified key areas of testimony and examples that would be offered. The witness indicated that they would have been willing to share it but none of the interpreters asked if such a document existed. This document would have been useful to the interpreters and points to additional questions that could have been asked in the preparation conversations.

Interpreter Interview Results

The interpreters in this study were also individually interviewed at the conclusion of the trials. The data reveal that the interpreters confirmed that forming a team is more than physically coming together to share the work. It requires a commitment to hold conversations pre- and post-trial, and to have strategies to address situations that can arise during their work. Two of the four interpreters reported that they have their preferred interpreters with whom they like to work, indicating that those interpreters have strong interpreting skills and similar working styles to their own. Two interpreters reported that when in their home communities, they often do not hold conversations prior to the work—They simply arrive and hope all goes well." The interpreters identified elements of their work that were successful as a team, and the one team acknowledged that because they had never worked together, and didn't know each other prior to this study, they struggled to work effectively and professionally with each other. This team had a significant disagreement during the interpretation, and when the interpreters were invited to reflect on why this may have occurred, one interpreter identified that s/he had formed an opinion of the other team member's competencies and/or lack of experience, and this affected her/his decision to continue interpreting for over one hour, believing the quality of her/his work was superior to the other interpreter's. This incident led to frustration between the two interpreters, along with feelings of anger and a sense of power imbalance. The Deaf witness reported that the incident led them to mistrust the team and it heightened his/her own anxiety about testifying. In this situation, had the interpreter honored the original agreement reached in the preparation conversation, and if the second interpreter had been more professionally assertive, this incident would not have occurred.

When asked about error correction, and the notion that working in teams results in increased accuracy, the interpreters reported that they felt they had managed the errors well and that the work was successful. However the analysis of the data showed several instances where team members did not correct the errors made by their colleague. This resulted in an inaccurate court record, and as with most mediated communication events, the consumers of the interpreting services are not in a position to know if the interpretation is accurate.

As reported in Russell (2002), there were numerous errors that were not corrected by the interpreters working in teams. Table 1 shows the number of interpreting errors per target language and by trial.

When error correction and the monitoring of each other's interpreting work was probed in the interviews, two responses were given: "I thought the interpreting WAS accurate and I agreed with my colleagues' interpreting," and "I knew they had it wrong, but I didn't think the error was significant to correct for the court."

These responses invite investigation about how to increase the abilities of interpreters to analyze their own work and about how court interpreters are trained in terms of ensuring the court has access to the most accurate record possible, regardless of how minor the correction may be.

By far the most relied upon strategies of all four interpreters when needing support from the monitor interpreter was to lean their upper torso or tilt their head towards that person in order to receive the spoken English feed. During the ASL to English work all four interpreters accepted support that was signed by the monitor interpreter but it was not clear in the data whether the interpreters asked for support, or if it was simply offered. The lawyers questioned the use of this behavior and were not sure what it meant between the two interpreters.

After the trials, the interpreters identified that they could have been more diligent in gaining preparation information from the expert witnesses and content specific information from the Crown prosecutor. If they had information in advance, it may have resulted in less conferring, or interpreter clarifications of the lawyers. For example, the team knew

TABLE 1. *Number of Interpreting Errors per Target Language and by Trial*

Discourse Event	Target Language	Trial 1–S*	Trial 2-C*	Trial 3-C	Trial 4-S
Expert Witness	ASL	21	5	27	32
Direct Evidence	ENG	22	3	3	27
Direct Evidence	ASL	17	1	3	18
Cross-Exam	ENG	7	0	1	7
Cross-Exam	ASL	8	1	2	9

* Note: "s" means simultaneous interpreting and "c" means consecutive interpreting

the charge being dealt with was sexual assault. However, they neglected to ask for the location where the alleged offense took place. In the trial the interpreters had to ask the Crown to repeat the name of the town, but had they asked for this information prior to the commencement of the trial there would have been no reason for the interruption.

All of the interpreters acknowledged that they lacked effective note-taking strategies, and that the notes they took did not support effective interpretation or effective teamwork. During one trial, the interpreters had to stop the proceedings in order to gather paper and pen as opposed to having it ready in case they needed the material.

IMPLICATIONS FOR INTERPRETERS WORKING IN TEAMS

Based on post-trial interviews, all the interpreters were able to identify aspects that could have been handled differently. All four interpreters acknowledged that there was content-specific information that they had neglected to ask of the Crown prosecutor. Upon reflection, the interpreters expressed concern that they had spent too much time attending to what was needed for the interpreting to go well and not enough time with some of the specifics of the trial.

While the interpreters met and prepared to act as a team in the interpreted interaction, after analyzing the data, there were unasked questions that may have been helpful to the teams. These questions may have reduced the impact of some of the errors that occurred in the trials and may have addressed some of the concerns expressed by the witnesses, lawyers, judges, and expert witness. The proposed questions include

- **How will we handle frozen text, such as oaths, in a consistent manner?** The interpreters did not share their interpretations for the oaths, which is text that is standard and predictable. The interpreters working during one trial had different versions of the oath for each time it was administered to the interpreters, the expert witness, and the Deaf witness.
- **What specific lexical choices might we need for this assignment?** The interpreters did not discuss with each other some of the specific lexical choices that arose in the trials, and had they done so it may have reduced the incidence of English-like signs, or source language intrusions that occurred in the English to ASL work.

- **What specific details of this case should we ask the lawyer to review with us?** This question could have been helpful in order to gain information about content or process. For example, the scope of the expert witness testimony, and the document that was submitted as an exhibit from this testimony was information that was available prior to the trial but the interpreters did not ask for it, so the lawyers did not provide it.
- **If we need to use notes during the trial, which one of us should take the notes and what symbols or structure would enhance the notes?** This question may have helped the interpreters find a better system for creating notes as opposed to the word-for-word strategy that was used in one of the trials. During trial three, one of the interpreters began taking notes while working with the expert witness. When the notes were examined after the trial, it was clear the majority of points were written verbatim from the spoken English. The interpreter then read the notes and presented the consecutive interpretation. The notes, when taken down in a verbatim fashion, actually interfered with providing meaning-based interpretation as when working from the notes, the interpreter's work demonstrated a greater tendency to follow the English grammatical structure and there were several source language intrusions based on the English. Prior to reverting to the note taking strategy, the interpreter's work was able to adhere to ASL grammatical principles and had fewer English source language intrusions.
- **Which one of us will tell the witness/lawyers about the purpose of the notes and how they will be destroyed at the end of the trial?** During the post-trial interview with the Deaf witnesses, both witnesses expressed concerns about the use of notes. While both Deaf witnesses were familiar with interpreting processes, neither of them had experienced interpreters taking notes during the interaction. The witnesses worried that the notes might be taken from the courtroom and be seen by others. For both Deaf witnesses, confidentiality was of paramount importance to them in all phases of the legal interaction, and they saw the notes as one possible breach of confidentiality if not disposed of properly.
- **If appropriate, what questions do we want to ask of the expert witness?** Three of the four interpreting teams held brief

conversations with the expert witness prior to the trials. However, in an interview with the expert witness after the conclusion of the trials, the witness expressed some concerns. First, one of the teams had not approached him/her at all, so the witness worried that the team would not understand the testimony, which then led to a reduced level of trust for the interpreting work of this team. Second, the witness also observed that two of the teams had engaged in the preparation conversation primarily from their perspective, focusing on the needs of the interpreters to the exclusion of the needs of the witness. Third, the expert witness had a summation document for the court, and had the interpreter asked about any documents or reports, the expert witness would have shared them with the interpreters. However, none of them inquired about this possibility. On a positive note, according to the expert witness, one interpreting team asked questions to determine the purpose of the testimony and areas of testimony that would be stressed in this trial, which led the witness to comment that he/she felt this team was creating a schema for the discourse that was about to take place in the courtroom.

DISCUSSION

This study involved four interpreters and as such, the results cannot be said to reflect all interpreters and nor are they intended to be generalized to a broader interpreter population. However, the study does provide rich information about preparation and team interpreting practices in this context. The four interpreters in this study are experienced practitioners, and yet the data reveals that the preparation conversations held with each other, and then with consumers were strongly oriented to the needs of the interpreters and overlooked aspects that were seen as crucial to consumers. While this study takes place in a legal context, it does suggest that there are opportunities for interpreters to carefully consider the perspectives of the consumers using their services and the context in which those services are provided in order to determine key questions that address the needs of the consumers. All of the consumers in this study have provided insight into questions that could have been posed that would have shaped the interaction in positive ways and these questions could easily become part of the interpreter's repertoire of preparation questions. It is interesting to note that several of the lawyers saw the interpreters as controlling and would have appreciated more of a dialogue preparation conversation versus what they perceived as a one-way monologue.

The judges in this study identified that they could have benefited from an orientation, either in print form, or through the crown prosecutor, prior to the trial. Several of the questions raised by the judges and lawyers stemmed from a misunderstanding of what the interpreters were attempting to do, especially in the area of error management and conferring between the interpreters. While the interpreters believed that they had addressed error management in their preparation conversations, from the lawyers' and judges' perspectives, this area was not effectively handled. There appear to be significant opportunities to examine the language and examples that interpreters use when attempting to describe their work and how they will perform in a given setting.

While Cokely (2003) reported that just 20% of the interpreters in that study identified linguistic or interpretation process issues that might create problems during the interpretation, in this study we see two out of the four interpreters address this area. It may be that the legal context created more awareness within the interpreters of the gravity of errors. However, as Cokely points out, it is highly desirable that such a discussion takes place as it helps to alert the monitor interpreter to potential areas where support might be needed. If all of the interpreters had been able to identify their linguistic and interpretation limitations, perhaps the error rate in this study would have been reduced by bringing the monitoring interpreter's attention to those aspects. The interpreters had introduced the concept of using a team as one vehicle to increasing the accuracy of the work, and yet there were significant errors that did occur and were not corrected by the team. As our field continues to document our practices it would be helpful to have comparable studies that examine the performance of interpreters working alone, so that comparisons could be made that would inform our evolving practice.

The conferring behavior aimed at error correction was visible across all trials, and may have been greater than is typical in an interpreting setting. For example, these interpreters were likely very sensitive to the nature of the study, and were more attentive to errors, and yet they were not able to address all of the significant errors. Thus it would seem that this area would be an important area to explore across a number of settings. Our dominant discourse has suggested that employing two interpreters will improve interpreting accuracy, and yet if we are not identifying our individual areas of linguistic and interpretation limitations, and we are not able to accurately monitor our work or the work of our colleagues, in practice, this may be a myth.

IMPLICATIONS FOR INTERPRETER EDUCATORS AND INTERPRETERS

There are several implications that emerge for the profession based on the results of this study, which could create opportunities for change. For interpreter educators, this is an opportunity to examine the ways in which we introduce interpreting in teams and the tools we provide to students in order to perform in an ethical and professional manner. This would lead to an evaluation of the curriculum focus we are using for team interpreting, and how we have integrated theory and practice. In this study it is noted that not all of the interpreters possessed strong linguistic analytical skills in order to assess their work and the work of their interpreter colleague. Educators would also assess the skills and competencies needed in order for interpreters to realistically monitor their own interpreting work and the work of their colleagues in a team. Further, there are opportunities to explore the ways in which educators model and teach problem solving and communication strategies that are a necessary part of effective team functioning. Finally, how interpreters prepare for the work has an impact on the end result, and this study has revealed additional aspects of preparation that could enhance courtroom interpreting, based on the multiple perspectives of our consumers.

CONCLUSION

This study reported the findings of preparation conversations held between interpreters, and among interpreters, lawyers, and Deaf witnesses. This study involved four interpreters and as such, the results cannot be said to reflect all interpreters and nor are they intended to be generalized to a broader interpreter population. However, the study does provide rich information about preparation and team interpreting practices in this context.

The experiences of signed language interpreters working in teams in order to provide effective mediated communication in an interpreted event reveal there are key issues to be addressed by teams prior to an event. In particular, interpreters need to have strategies for managing team communication and problem solving during and after interpreting assignments if consumers are to be well served. The four experienced interpreters in this study held conversations with each other, prior to the interpreted event, addressing their preferences for working together in order to provide an effective service. The interpreters then held preparation conversations with consumers, both Deaf and non-deaf. These conversations reveal that interpreters may in fact overwhelm consumers with details about the specific nature of linguistic and cultural approaches to interpretation, while completely missing the issues of importance for consumers.

Several themes emerged from the interviews held with participants after the interpreted events. For interpreters, themes of trust, assessment of colleagues' capabilities, and power issues between team members were highlighted. For Deaf consumers, the key themes that emerged focused on the lack of professionalism observed in some instances and the ways in which that may affect the consumers' ability to trust the team to convey their narratives in a way that will allow them to be heard by the lawyers and the judges in the study. Finally, the key themes from interviews with the judges and the lawyers centered on ways in which they did not understand the work of the interpreters and the questions they needed answered in order to feel comfortable with the interpreters prior to beginning the trials.

In addition, the study raises challenges to the prevailing notions or myths that have shaped our field like the notion that a team of interpreters ensures consumers will have the most effective and accurate interpretations. This study shows that interpreters are not, in fact, consistently monitoring each other's work and making corrections to work. Nor is it the case that all interpreters are functioning well as teams, and that does not go unnoticed by Deaf consumers, thus shaping future relationships with interpreters.

The results that are highlighted in this study invite further dialogue among interpreters about the kinds of conversations that should shape our preparation conversations and the ways in which those conversations can be held with consumers in order to address the pressing questions they have about working with signed language interpreters. Educators have opportunities to examine the ways in which newcomers to the field are introduced to the concept of team interpreting, and the ways in which they can influence future practice. By addressing some of the myths and modeling different strategies that engender trust and that support effective interpretation, we will continue to ensure consumers are well served by the interpretation provided.

Finally, this study invites further research for comparative studies across various interpreting settings. There are many questions that emerge that would be helpful in order to advance our profession and to increase our capacity to build our teaching and interpreting practices on solid research and evidence. For example, how do consumers view language fluency as a measure of interpreting competence? Many of the errors that emerged in this study were errors of ASL to English comprehension, and yet Deaf consumers expressed confidence in the interpreters based on their use of ASL. What do lawyers and judges perceive as appropriate preparation and how that can be ethically gathered? What skills are needed by interpreters in order to effectively monitor their own interpreting processes and performances, prior to working as a monitor of another interpreter's performance? This study examined the work of four interpreters in a legal context, and there is increasing use of Deaf interpreters to work with non-deaf interpreters in such settings. What kinds of team related issues arise when forming such a team?

This study offers evidence-based research findings that should help shape the practices of interpreters who work in teams, and hold preparation conversations. It may also serve as a starting place for learning conversations that could be held among novice and experienced practitioners who wish to improve their team interpreting performance across a multitude of settings.

REFERENCES

Association of Visual Language Interpreters of Canada. (2000). The Association of Visual Language Interpreters' code of ethics and guidelines for professional conduct. Retrieved August 12, 2008, from http://www.avlic.ca/ethics.htm on.

Cokely, D. (2003). Interpreting in teams: A pilot study on requesting and offering support. *Journal of Interpretation* (pp. 49–93). Alexandria, VA: Registry of Interpreters for the Deaf.

Demers, H. (2005). The working interpreter. In T. Janzen (Ed.), *Topics in signed language interpreting* (pp. 203–230). Amsterdam: John Benjamins.

Frishberg, N. (1986). *Interpreting: An introduction.* Alexandria, VA: Registry of Interpreters for the Deaf.

Miles, M., & Huberman, M. (1994). *An expanded sourcebook: Qualitative data analysis.* Thousand Oaks, CA: Sage.

Pöchacker, F. (2004). *Introducing interpreting studies.* London: Routledge.

Registry of Interpreters for the Deaf. (2005). NAD-RID code of ethics. Retrieved from August 12, 2008, http://www.rid.org/UserFiles/File/pdfs/codeofethics.pdf on.

Russell, D. (2000). *Interpreting in legal contexts: Consecutive and simultaneous interpretation.* Burtonsville, MD: Linstok Press.

Russell, D. (2005). Consecutive and simultaneous interpreting. In T. Janzen (Ed.), *Topics in signed language interpreting* (pp. 135–164). Amsterdam: John Benjamins.

Shaw, Risa (2003). *Monitoring interpretations: Analysis, discretion and collaboration.* Paper presented at the Conference of Legal Sign Language Interpreters annual meeting, Atlanta, GA.

Solow, S. (2000). *Sign language interpreting: A basic resource text* (Rev. ed.). Silver Spring, MD: National Association of the Deaf.

Stewart, D., Schein. J., & Cartwright, B. (2005). *Sign language interpreting—Exploring its art and science.* Boston: Allyn and Bacon.

Wadensjö, C. (1998). *Interpreting as interaction.* London: Longman.

Wilcox, S., & Shaffer, B. (2005). Towards a cognitive model of interpreting. In T. Janzen (Ed.), *Topics in signed language interpreting* (pp. 27–50). Amsterdam: John Benjamins.

Witter-Merithew, A., & Johnson, L. (2005). *Toward competent practice: Conversations with stakeholders.* Alexandria, VA: Registry of Interpreters for the Deaf.

Legal Interpreting and the Deaf Community in Malaysia

Zubaidah Ibrahim-Bell

In the more economically developed countries of the world, a good deal of progress has been made in raising social awareness of the nature and functions of signed languages and signed language interpreting (SLI), providing signed language courses and signed language interpreter training, and creating registers of qualified and certified interpreters.[1]

The same cannot yet be said of the majority of less developed countries including Malaysia where, in spite of considerable effort, much remains to be done.[2] This stems partly from inadequate resources and partly from the fact that there are two competing forms of signed language in use in the country: one recognized and promoted by the state and taught to deaf children in special schools; the other the language of choice of the Deaf community as a whole.

This chapter begins with a description of the language setting in Malaysia, followed by the situation of signed language (SL) interpreters in the Deaf community in Malaysia, with a special focus on SL interpreters in legal contexts and on, in particular, the issues related to legal interpreting and the problems the SL interpreters routinely experience working in a wide range of legal settings. The description draws on general information provided by the incumbent president of the Malaysian Foundation for the Deaf and on data obtained from a small questionnaire-based study conducted in 2007.

I wish to thank Lucy Lim-Yip for her invaluable assistance and cooperation in the collection of data for this study.

1. The Register of Public Service Interpreters held and administered by the Chartered Institute of Linguistics in the United Kingdom is a well-known example: http://www.iol.org.uk.

2. South Africa is a notable exception: see Deaf Federation of South Africa (DEAFSA).

SETTING: LANGUAGES IN MALAYSIA

Malaysia consists of three major communities which, between them, account for some 90% of the total population: Malay (60%); Chinese (25%); Indian (5%) and several minor communities ranging from indigenous groups (about 6%), particularly in East Malaysia, through several different migrant groups (about 4%) to Deaf people (perhaps 0.01%).[3]

Using standard language planning terminology, Malaysia can be classified as an *endoglossic* state in which the mother tongue of the largest speech community (Malay: *Bahasa Malaysia:* BM) has been adopted as the official language of the country with a Type B language policy: the choice of an indigenous language to act as the symbol of national unity and the vehicle for creating and sustaining solidarity in the state.[4] The language profile of Malaysia can be summarized as follows.[5]

1. One official language (*Bahasa Malaysia/Melayu* or Malay: the language of the majority indigenous community).
2. One promoted language (English, the language of the former colonial power).
3. Three supported languages: Mandarin and Tamil—the dominant languages of the Chinese and Indian communities, respectively and KTBM which is manually coded BM; one of the varieties of sign available to Deaf people. To this should now be added *Bahasa Isyarat Malaysia* (BIM), Malaysian Signed Language (MySL), previously a tolerated language.
4. At least three languages of public worship: Arabic, Sanskrit, and Pali.
5. A number of tolerated languages that are recognized to exist but are neither proscribed nor supported by the authorities.

3. Figures from BBC International News; Country Profile: Malaysia. Retrieved from http://news.bbc.co.uk/2/hi/asia-pacific/country_profiles on August 12, 2008.

4. The terms are, with the exception of "supported language" (which is newly coined for this paper), from Kloss (1968) (see Bell, 1976, pp. 168–174 for further discussion).

5. The profile represents the national situation: individual states may well have different profiles such as Iban in East Malaysia which would be categorized as promoted.

These would include not only the languages of the aboriginal *orang asli* of West Malaysia and the 30 or more languages of migrant workers but also the socially important *Bahasa Pasar* (Bazaar Malay), which provides an alternative inter- and, even, intragroup lingua franca.[6]

Bahasa Malaysia (BM) provides the communication link between the citizen and the state. It is the medium of instruction in state schools and tertiary institutions, the language of trial and record in the courts, and an intergroup lingua franca. The general public is expected to use Malay in most of their dealings with the authorities, including the courts, the police, and the medical services. Where contact cannot be established through BM, interpreters (not necessarily, and rarely, trained or experienced individuals) are made (or make themselves) available.

English performs a similar role to BM, facilitating some intergroup communication (e.g., between speakers of different Indian languages) and intragroup communication within speech communities unwilling or unable to make adequate use of BM (e.g., some professional groups in particular domains), and much international communication (Malaysia is an export-led economy). It is used widely in business and commerce alongside Chinese dialects, Tamil, and other Indian languages in their respective communities.

With the exception of the courts, there is virtually no organized public service interpreting in Malaysia. The need is typically met by ad hoc interpreting by individuals who are either bilingual service providers (e.g., a doctor or police officer who speaks Malay and another language) or family members or friends who consider their control of both languages to be adequate enough to provide ad hoc interpreting services. There is a small amount of conference interpreting, which is provided by experienced but untrained freelancers typically at international meetings. The language pairs, however, tend not to include Malay, since Malaysian academics and other professionals are most likely to present and engage in discussion in such situations in English.

Deaf people are unable to use any of the country's spoken languages and have to acquire or learn some form of sign language if they are not to be totally excluded not only from the life of the rest of their nation

6. Bazaar Malay (literally, "market language") is an institutionalized pidgin lingua franca of long-standing (see esp. Collins, 1987) still used by many of the older generation of the Chinese and Indian communities.

but even from their own families. For them, contact with society outside their own community depends entirely on those who can interpret between spoken languages and signed language.

SIGNED LANGUAGE INTERPRETING (SLI)

Interpreting, whether between spoken or signed languages, always occurs in a social context and involves, minimally, a sender who transmits messages in one language and a receiver who converts the messages from that language into another for the benefit of a client who does not share the sender's language.

Seen in these terms, translation and interpreting both require a language switch and differ only in the medium they employ—the visual versus the aural/oral—and the time required for carrying out the process; translation normally takes more time than interpreting (whether consecutive or simultaneous). Further, speech-to-speech and speech-to-sign interpreting can also be distinguished in terms of medium: oral/aural versus oral/visual.

An informal estimate provided by the Majudiri Y Foundation, an affiliate of the YMCA Kuala Lumpur (MYF, 2006, pp. 82–83) suggests that there are at most 100 SL interpreters in the country. However, many of these are literate Deaf people who interpret between the idiosyncratic, nonstandard signed or gesture systems of illiterate Deaf individuals and standard KTMB or BIM;[7] others are hearing people who can sign and are familiar with Deaf culture. Very rarely do any of these interpreters have formal qualifications in SLI. A report in an online journal (*4HearingLoss,* 2006) stated that there are currently only seven qualified and trained SL interpreters in Malaysia, concentrated in the Klang Valley around the capital.

This is clearly a grossly inadequate provision in a nation with a registered deaf population of 27,000, particularly since Deaf people need assistance in a large number of domains: job interviews, seminars and conferences, counseling, medical appointments, social events such as wedding receptions, and legal matters including court trial proceedings.

7. The term *illiterate* is used to refer to Deaf persons who are unable to communicate in a recognized signed language or a manual version of a spoken language.

Interpreters in Malaysian Courts

Most trials are conducted in Malay, the official language of trial and of record. This creates a problem when the accused person or witness wishes to give evidence in a language other than Malay. With sizeable linguistic minorities in the population and substantial numbers of non-Malay-speaking migrant workers, interpreters are inevitably required to facilitate trials.

The variety of standard Malay used in court is a highly specialized register with its own legal terminology and unique meanings that are not readily understood by a layperson. An individual may be fluent in Bazaar Malay but unable to deal with the language of the court, either in understanding the proceedings or making a response. In terms of common law, international law, and natural justice, such an individual needs and is entitled to an interpreter because a fair trial requires the full understanding and participation of the accused.

> The Federal Constitution and the Criminal Procedure Code (CPC 270) both assert the right of an individual to the services of an interpreter, if s/he is involved in a court appearance, as accused, litigant, defendant, or witness, and does not speak Malay well enough to take part in the proceedings.

> Whenever any evidence is given in a language not understood by the accused, and he is present in person, it shall be interpreted to him in open court in a language that he understands. (CPC 1997, ch. 25, cl. 270, p. 85)

However, one exceptional feature of the Malaysian court is that there is no court stenographer, clerk, or mechanical device to keep a record of the proceedings and no audio or video recordings may be made by third parties. The presiding officer in the High Court is required by the CPC to make notes in his own hand. "In all criminal cases tried before the High Court the Judge shall take down in writing notes of the evidence adduced" (CPC, ch. 6, sec. 272).

This practice has carried through to the lower courts with the result that, in addition to slowing down the proceedings and leaving only a summary record, it precludes the collection of any of the kind of data essential for the study of courtroom discourse. The researcher is left only with the option of attempting to make written notes in real time of the actual exchanges that take place in a trial and, clearly, for signed language exchanges in particular, this is not feasible.

Accepting the need for an SL interpreter is not an issue, as it can be with spoken language, especially when an individual's Bazaar Malay is considered to be adequate for participation in the proceedings. It is automatically recognized that a deaf person requires an interpreter. Mere recognition does not, however, solve the problem. The decision has to be implemented. This requires the location of a speaking person who (a) can sign, (b) can function as an interpreter in court, and (c) is qualified (or deemed to be qualified).

SL Interpreters in Legal Contexts

Legal interpreting is a variety of public service interpreting, since it provides a communication link between state or national agencies and individuals (and communities) whose rights to public services are compromised by their inadequate command of the national language(s).

Legal interpreting is accepted to refer to a much wider setting than just the courtroom (Colin & Morris, 1996; Gammal, 2003; Mikkelson, 2000) and includes all the stages and locations in the judicial process such as interviews in police stations with accused and/or witnesses, lawyer-client meetings in the lawyer's office or a remand center, hearings in chambers, and trial hearings in open court.

In Malaysia, mediated links between the individual and the state are rarely found outside the law and, within that, the courtroom setting of the trial itself. Most pre-trial, social, and medical interpreting is taken on in an ad hoc manner by bilinguals who consider mere bilingualism to be sufficient qualification for providing such a service. The Deaf community in Malaysia, however, is more broadly covered, with SL interpreters not only serving in court but also in hospitals, at social functions, in police stations, lawyers' offices, and judges' chambers.

Interpreting in court is perhaps the most difficult, complex, and stressful of all types of interpreting. The trial process itself is intricately complex with its specialist terminology and subtle usages, its rules of evidence, precedence and procedure, the content of legal texts underlying the argument, and the subject matter of the case and the irreversible consequences to the parties involved if mistakes are made and communication is faulty. All of these complexities tend to create stress in the interpreter. The added particular difficulties of SLI often lead, understandably, to interpreters' feelings of inadequacy and emotional exhaustion.

DESCRIPTION OF THE STUDY

Informants and Issues

A short survey was conducted early in 2007. Two questionnaires were created and sent out via e-mail: one for the Malaysian Foundation for the Deaf (MFD), which was answered by its president, and a second one for SL interpreters who were members of the MFD and the MYF, two nongovernmental organizations.

All the interpreters are hearing signers who have acquired signed language through their own contacts with the Deaf community. However, the degree of training and the range of language competence they display vary greatly as shown in Table 1. All seven have interpreted for Deaf people in a wide range of situations; formal and informal and within and outside the community. All except one (B) have also interpreted in legal settings, including the open courts.

TABLE 1. *Respondents to the Questionnaire*

Interpreter	Qualifications	Experience in Legal interpreting
A	Certificate in SL Interpreter Training (Grant McEwan Community College)	Yes
B	B.A. (currently pursuing a post-graduate degree)	No
C	B.A.	Yes
D	Teaching certificate	Yes
E	Teaching certificate	Yes
F	School certificate, local Chinese dialects; adequate English	Yes
G	School certificate, Malay only	Yes

The first questionnaire (aimed at the interpreters) is divided into four sections:

1. Respondents' background of SL education.
2. Their personal experience as SL interpreters.
3. Their views and opinions on interpreting in court in general.
4. The exchanges that they found significant, problematic, and/or interesting.

All of them admit that they have not recorded any of these experiences in any way previously. When asked to detail their experiences for this study, it took them a long time to respond. For this reason, what is conveyed is either general impressions and examples or extreme instances they remember vividly. However, asking the questions triggered a process of reflection that has led to a number of the respondents writing later to elaborate on their experiences and add more comments outside the questionnaire format.

The main purpose of the survey was to find out (1) what kind of cases involving members of the Deaf community are brought before the courts, (2) the competence and qualifications of the interpreters who take on the role of intermediary between the Deaf and the hearing communities, and (3) the problem areas that they encounter.

The motivation for the investigation is to find information that can be incorporated into the training of SL interpreters and contribute to the establishment of the interpreting profession in Malaysia. The sample is necessarily limited due to the small number of SL interpreters in the country but, in that sense, it is a good representation of the current SL interpreter population.

The information that the researcher requested from the MFD president, who is deaf, is data on the Deaf community, the training and educational programs offered to Deaf people, the perception of the public toward the Deaf community, the issue of the signed language preferred by Deaf people (as this at times became quite an emotional subject among the Deaf associations), and the attitude toward professional training for interpreters.

According to the MFD president, Deaf people were more often than not paid less than hearing workers. This situation is changing rapidly as more and more Malaysian Deaf people are going abroad for qualifications that are not available in Malaysia, acquiring skills that allow them to receive the same pay as comparably qualified and experienced hearing workers. One result of this has been an increase in the demand for SL interpreters. At the same time, the interpreters do not receive formal training on how to work with the Deaf community.

For this reason, the MFD has established a training center, staffed by professional individuals who will create and implement a program leading to standards that are recognized by the Malaysian government. The MFD president seems optimistic that the recent funding granted will enable the foundation to set up and run assessment and accreditation procedures:

> Berkaitan dengan kelayakan seorang itu menjadi jurubahasa isyarat atau pentauliahannya, Persatuan Juru Bahasa Isyarat Malaysia dan Persekutuan kami akan bertanggungjawab untuk mengadakan peperiksaan penilaian. Kerajaan Malaysia melalui Bajet 2007 juga memperuntukkan menubuhkan pusat latihan yang ada sekarang. (Mohamad Sazali Shaari, e-mail communication, May 31, 2007)
>
> [As to the qualifications to be a signed language interpreter, . . . our Federation will be responsible for preparing for assessment examinations. The Malaysian Government through its 2007 Budget has also allocated funding for the formal establishment of a training centre.] (author translation)

RESULTS OF THE QUESTIONNAIRE TO INTERPRETERS

The responses and feedback were analyzed qualitatively under four major headings to reflect the concerns of the interpreters related to legal interpreting. These are (a) competence, including the interpreter's formal training and qualifications, and the role of teachers as interpreters; (b) illiterate participants: witnesses and defendants; (c) the multiple roles of the interpreter; and (d) professional concerns and good practice. After the issues are introduced, the relevant responses are reported, followed by comments and discussion after each response.

With regard to the kind of legal cases that involve Deaf people, most interpreters reported that they were required to mediate in divorce settlements (usually in lawyers' offices), petty thefts, shoplifting, copyright infringement (mainly selling pirated CDs and DVDs), illegal drug consumption, and traffic offenses (usually in magistrates' courts). The rape case mentioned in this study involved a Deaf student who was the victim of her own teacher, a hearing person.

Competence

It is commonly accepted that in terms of competence, a legal interpreter needs to (a) be highly proficient in the languages concerned (and this includes an ability to manipulate registers); (b) have gone through a program of formal training; and (c) acquired a certification in all the aspects involved in interpreting: linguistic, specialist knowledge, and technique (Gonzalez et al., 1991; de Jongh, 1992; Edwards, 1995).

However, it appears that worldwide, courts often compromise best practice in the case of foreign language interpreters (and in Malaysia, SL interpreters as well) by taking on individuals who have no formal training in legal procedure or interpreting (see Mikkelson, 2000; Moeketsi, 1999; Morris, 1995).

Not only do the courts often rely on bilingual individuals who are incompetent but also many judges and attorneys are unaware of the interpreter's professional responsibilities. This is in striking contrast with many of the interpreters themselves, who are aware and concerned about their own performance in court. The legal professionals' lack of concern over standards is evident even in the initial swearing in of the interpreter. All that is required is for the interpreter to declare on oath that s/he will "tell the truth." Next s/he merely asserts that s/he is proficient in the languages concerned. For the SL interpreter hired by lawyers, the requirement is even less stringent:

> Sadly the Courts are not particular about qualifications, the lawyers just need to inform [the court] that the victim is Deaf and that they have brought their own interpreter etc. We are usually asked to give our name card and also IC [Identification Card] as identification. Since I have my certificate, I usually make a copy and submit it to the court for their record . . . (A)

> The Court readily accepts the use of signed language interpreters without checking their credentials, years of experience, or whether they have any training. They just record our IC number and our name . . . (C)

Similarly, in the lawyer's office, the interpreter's credentials are not required.

At times a trained and experienced interpreter will have to deal with an untrained interpreter from the other party during an interpreting session. This can put the trained interpreter in an embarrassing position. On the one hand, s/he recognizes the responsibility for ensuring that the facts are correctly transmitted and recorded and, on the other, will feel a sense of solidarity with the other interpreter. In the following, the certified SL interpreter A describes what occurred during a session in a lawyer's office.

> During the discussion with the lawyers, it was apparent that the interpreter for Mr. X made several grave mistakes in her voicing skills [sic].
>
> The lawyer asked: So you will pay a monthly maintenance of RM 250 for your child. (This was signed by the interpreter.)
>
> Mr. X signed: I don't think I can afford it. Let me think about it.
>
> (The interpreter did not voice this for him.)
>
> The lawyer took it that Mr. X agreed to the monthly statement, since there was no answer from him . . . He then made notes.
>
> I was very uneasy as I wasn't sure if I should intervene, since this was the interpreter that he had brought himself. The conversation went on for several minutes and after the third time the lawyer stated the fact that Mr. X will pay maintenance and yet still interpreter did not voice his reply . . . I decided to intervene.
>
> I asked the permission of Mrs. X if it is OK to clear matters in this discussion. She said OK. I then asked Mr. X if it is OK if I can clarify the question asked by the lawyer and that his Interpreter did not voice for him.
>
> He looked surprised and I explained the matter to him and he agreed for me to voice what he had signed earlier to his lawyer.

The lawyer was surprised and quickly made changes in his notes.

Mrs. X then said she didn't want any maintenance from Mr. X. She just wanted the divorce. The matter then was settled.

In the absence of any specification for qualified interpreters, the courts often display a distrust of non-civil servant interpreters and tend to prefer teachers of the Deaf, as fellow civil servants, to interpret for them.

In some cases that I know of, there are a number of teachers who have been called to interpret for court cases. These are teachers from the outskirts like Perak, Kedah, and Penang because the Police and the Courts think that since they are teachers of the Deaf, they are deemed qualified to interpret . . . (A)

I also found out lately that the Court will only accept Signed Language Interpreters if they are civil servants—this means they only choose Teachers from the Deaf Schools to interpret in Court. They reason that NGO's are biased so they prefer civil servants . . . (C)

Jurubahasa isyarat Mahkamah bukan perkara atau tugas yang senang, kami memerlukan kefahaman dari pelbagai Pihak, iaitu Pengguna, Peguam dan Hakim. Maka sikap yang berkecuali kami kadang kala telah salah ditafsirkan . . . (G)

[Being a courtroom signed language interpreter is not easy; we need their understanding, that is from the Consumer [*sic*], Lawyer and Judge. Our impartial attitude is sometimes misconstrued.] (G [author translation])

However, observations from the respondents—interpreters, teachers, and representatives of the NGO alike—all report that the teachers encounter major problems functioning as legal interpreters.

I experienced a lot of problems, to do with signing skills . . . (E)

It's a tough job. Interpreters must be alert and must know very well the terms used by the court . . . (D)

> Walaupun terdapatnya guru sekolah Pekak menjadi jurubahasa di mahkamah, namun kami mempertikaikan kemampuan mereka . . . (G)
>
> [Even though there are teachers of Deaf schools who function as interpreters in the courts, we question their ability.] (G, [author translation])

There seem to be two explanations for this situation: a series of interlinked misconceptions based on what might be labeled the "naïve language user fallacy" and the "literal fallacy" respectively (Bell, 2007).

The first holds to the naïve assumption that all bilingual people can translate and interpret and, in particular, that all language service provider roles are interchangeable; not only can all language teachers teach, they can also translate and interpret; and all translators can also teach and interpret and all interpreters can teach and translate.

The second fallacy assumes that accurate translation (and interpreting) must be literal and, since KTBM is the official language of the Deaf and its syntax lends itself easily to word-for-word translation, those who use it are more acceptable to the court than those who do not. The courts seem immovable on their insistence that interpreters translate every word in the same order as the original. They believe it is not the place of the interpreter to interpret. Interpretation is the preserve of the judiciary. The interpreter is, in the classic model, a mere conduit who in no way participates in the process other than to carry messages over from a speaker to a listener.

Equally, the courts are used to working with their own resident interpreters, who are civil servants, and who are perceived to be impartial (see Ibrahim 2007). For this reason, other civil servants (the teachers of the Deaf) are more preferred and are hired on a case by case basis. SL interpreters, on the other hand, are perceived to be partial and have a closeness with their Deaf clients.

Legal professionals might also have a stereotypical view of signed languages as pidgin versions of real languages rather than languages in their own right. The dominant position of KTMB in Malaysia and the preference of teachers for that rather than BIM would seem very likely to strengthen the stereotype.

Such misconceptions among judges and court officers about the ability of teachers of the Deaf to act as competent interpreters are by no means limited to Malaysia.[8]

Illiterate Participants

Interpreters report that if the Deaf individuals are proficient in BIM, the interpreting sessions, whether at the lawyers' office or in court, will be smooth.

> Both consecutive and simultaneous interpreting was used for this session as both of them are educated and are good in their command of BIM . . . (A)

However, very often, deaf people who appear at court, whether as defendant or witness, have not learned any signed language. Families are embarrassed by having a deaf member and often keep them at home, or the family is too poor to send the deaf family member to a special school.

A trained and experienced interpreter will resort to other methods to help such a person understand and participate in the proceedings. The information reported below illustrates how such an interpreter is able to deal with an illiterate client, even if only to inform him about his conviction and sentence. In contrast, interpreters who are not trained found it difficult.

> Mr. X was illiterate and I had to use lots of gestures, role play in court. On one occasion I had to draw so that he could understand, especially when the court passed the sentence that he will be jailed for two and half years . . . (A)

> The victim or witnesses or even defendant are illiterate. Is not an easy job. Must be very skilful in all aspects . . . (E)

> Ya, banyak masalah dengan orang Pekak yang tidak faham dengan istilah Undang- undang. Jurubahasa terpaksa mengubah kepada bahasa yang mudah difahami (G)

8. See Court Interpretation: Model Guide for Policy and Practice. Retrieved from www.ncsconline.org/ on August 12, 2008.

[Yes, a lot of problems with the Deaf persons who don't understand legal terminology, interpreters have to change to another language [sic] so they can easily understand.] (G, [author translation])

The Deaf person was quite illiterate so I had to do a lot of consecutive interpreting, lots of drawings, lots of repetition. For this case I used the consecutive mode as my deaf client is weak in Signed Language and he comes from Ipoh, not Kuala Lumpur. So I actually don't know him well enough to be comfortable with his signing styles. I also used a lot of visual expression, and body language due to his limited signs. (A)

An accused Deaf person who is illiterate is unlikely to understand what is taking place in the court and will be unable to plead. In such circumstances, a fair trial cannot take place. A frequent solution is to employ two interpreters who operate a relay system, the first converting the deaf person's idiosyncratic signs into standard signs and then the second interpreting those signs into speech, and the converse. However, to use a team of interpreters may be seen as a luxury, for which the permission of the court needs to be obtained, as the rape case reported below confirms.

The case, which involved a deaf child in a residential school, was brought to the attention of a Deaf organization and a local non-governmental organization, the Sabah Association of Women (SAWO). Together they took action on behalf of the victim by reporting the incident to the police and having the case brought to court. The prosecution was successful. According to the interpreter

The rapist got 18 years and five strokes of the *rotan* on this first charge.[9] [For the] second, with the same child, he got 18 years and five strokes of the *rotan*. The sentences were to run concurrently. . . . For the second child that he raped, he got 18 years in jail and 12 strokes of the *rotan*. This sentence to run after the first two. We believe the first case in which he was found guilty set a precedent for the other case as well. . . . One of the things we asked for is that two Signed Language Interpreters be provided: a Deaf Interpreter and a Hearing Signed Language Interpreter. Our argument

9. *Rotan* is the instrument used in flogging, which is still used in judicial corporal punishment in Malaysia and Singapore.

> is that the Victim is a child and has minimal language skills. Another was for a screen to save the child from having to see the "rapist" who also happen to be a teacher of the Deaf. (A)

In the above case, the request to have two signed language interpreters allocated to the prosecution was actually contested by the defense lawyers but accepted by the bench. The social worker involved and the members of SAWO, some of whom were lawyers themselves, saw this as a victory and considered themselves lucky to have been given permission to use two interpreters.

In the United States, the Registry for Interpreters of the Deaf (RID) allows for a general practice of collaborations among interpreters (RID, 2005). There are several arguments in support of this; legal assignments are more complex than other kinds of assignments and one interpreter should watch the other to ensure the accuracy of the interpreting. Members of the Deaf community differ both in terms of their communicative competence and their communication needs and for the illiterate Deaf person such relay interpreting is absolutely essential.

Police stations, however, obtain interpreters from within their own force and, failing that, from others who are known to speak the language required. None of these people are formally trained, much less certified. For cases involving deaf witnesses and defendants, the same procedure is followed, as reported below.

> Usually the courts don't contact us . . . it's the Police station that look for us . . . I once ask the Brickfields police how they get us. They said if there are problems in looking for translators they will contact each other. For example, if they need to get a statement out of a Chinese-speaking man who only speaks Mandarin, then they will send out a notice to all the Police stations around the district to identify an officer who can speak that "dialect." Similarly all the Police stations will be notified if they have a special case (for example involving the Deaf) and usually the Brickfields Police station will respond, because they know the YMCAs do have people who work with the Deaf . . . (A)

The Malaysian courts normally provide for three interpreters for each court to interpret between Malay and English, Malay/English and Chinese (Mandarin and dialects), and Malay/English and the Indian languages, as required. In East Malaysia, the interpreters usually speak the local languages and dialects and interpret between these and English/Malay. When a foreign language is involved, the court resorts to its list of interpreters who are bilingual people from the embassies, language centers, and other individuals known to be proficient in the language.

Multiple Roles

Much like the spoken language interpreter, the SL interpreter is often expected to be more than an interpreter. In different contexts, and even in one single interpreting sitting, they may function as confidante, co-worker, assistant, advocate, and counselor. They are often faced with conflicts and dilemmas that wear them down.

> After it was over . . . I felt terrible . . . I did not go back to work. Instead went home to sleep and rest. This case was an emotional one for me and I'm not sure if I should have interpreted. . . . We wear many hats. Since I am also a "social worker" of the Deaf, I have to assist them with this and that.(A)

> Most of us signed language interpreters know our clients very well, sometimes since they were young. Being small in numbers, it is very difficult for us to avoid some of these cases as we know it would be difficult for them to have their case heard if there are no interpreters available.(C)

> I was not treated as a signed language interpreter but more on a help basis to settle cases [*sic*]. (D)

One ever-present danger is that of sliding into the advocate role and thereby breaching the interpreters' code of ethics.

> At the very outset I had to make very clear to Maya (the Lawyer) that I was there to serve Debra (a Deaf person) as Debra had engaged me and she was my client. While I played the neutral role in the four discussions, I found myself at times leaning in support towards Debra. Outside of my interpreting for her, we used to meet and I would lend an ear to her. I needed to understand this woman and what she was going through without being judgmental. (C)

Sometimes I feel in the interpretation for divorce cases there is interference from family members who make decisions for them (the clients). (A)

The context of the interpreting setting greatly influences the behavior of the participants and the way in which the process itself is carried out. For example, the exchanges between a lawyer and a Deaf client located in the lawyer's office are likely to be mediated in a more relaxed way than if they were taking place in a police station, a judge's chambers, or in the courtroom due to the formal surroundings. In a lawyer's office, an interpreter may not be just a mouthpiece but have more empathy for their client.

Professional Concerns and Good Practice

In a courtroom, the interpreter is faced with different sets of problems: the norms regulating the use of legal language and the court's discourse conventions;, the expectations that these norms give rise to; the tension among individuals and role-players in the power hierarchy of the court; the interplay between the possession of differential status, power, and prestige; the clash between the legal culture and the larger society; and the greater clash between the culture of the court and the culture of the accused/litigant/witness for whom the interpreter is acting as a link and mediator (see Bell, 1976, p.102 for a model of the relationships among status, prestige, role, norm, code, and domain). The interpreters are well aware of such issues.

When I do legal interpreting, I myself am not aware of some of the legal words and laws pertaining to each of the cases. (C)

I was prepared for the situation and thus brought my own *tudung* and wear a *baju kurung* as a mark of respect to the court and to the Muslim law,[10] but . . . many times, during the proceedings Arabic words were used and in many occasions, this was interpreted in English by the Magistrate himself for me . . . looking back I'm not sure if I had been effective since I'm not a Muslim and was not able to understand the depth of some of the Arabic words used. (A)

10. A head covering and a modest, traditional Malay dress.

> Sad to say . . . the Deaf guy, Mr. Tong does not come to talk to me anymore . . . I have a feeling he feels embarrassed that I know his stories. . . . He married his second wife and, yes, I was not invited. . . . His second wife who is also Deaf, does talk to me . . . oh well . . . the hazards of being an interpreter in a small community. (A)

All of the interpreters have had the experience of being treated as volunteers and not being paid a professional rate for their work. One interpreter remarked that SL interpreters are seen as doing social work and therefore do not get paid. One interpreter reported

> When a lawyer calls me to interpret for a Deaf individual, I normally do not like to go unless they pay me earlier [i.e., in advance]. Lawyers cannot be trusted; they might not want to pay after I did the job. I have been conned [sic] a couple of times. (F)

Such treatment is a stark contrast to the way lawyers hired by Deaf clients expect to be treated. They expect to be paid professional fees, plus traveling expenses if they are required to leave their office.

> When one engages a lawyer, it's not always clear how much money you will end up paying the lawyer. The lawyer can come up with an estimate of legal fees but disbursements and other miscellaneous administration costs cannot be determined all the time. . . . Each time you call a lawyer out to meet you at different locations, someone has to pay for her expenses. (C)

CONCLUSION AND RECOMMENDATIONS

This short study reveals that SL interpreters in legal contexts in Malaysia are in a much worse situation than spoken language interpreters in terms of recognition, training, and remuneration. Based on their responses, only one (who has professional qualifications) of the seven SL interpreters seems confident and resourceful when interpreting in court. The other five reported encountering difficulties and one (Interpreter B) did not even attempt to do it. At present, a specialized SL training for legal settings is nonexistent though general SL courses are being offered by the Deaf associations.

The Deaf community stands out from others in the extent to which all its members are marginalized and potentially at risk. From the point of view of linguistics, the community offers boundless scope for research: both fundamental research into SL usage and applied research into ways of helping the community improve its communication links with the hearing world.

Fundamental research could be carried out on the formal and functional characteristics of the linguistic codes used in the community (the syntax, semantics, and pragmatics); discourse practices in face-to-face encounters between Deaf participants and between Deaf and hearing individuals; variation between and within codes (dialect and register); communication networks (intra- and intercommunity); degrees of bilingualism; childhood acquisition, and more.

Applied research could be carried out most profitably at the interface between the Deaf and the hearing worlds and, most particularly, on the teaching and acquisition of signed languages and the education of interpreters.

The existing network of SL service providers is indisputably inadequate, disorganized, and physically scattered across the country, with the providers themselves lacking formal qualifications. What is needed next is to develop and expand this network into a recognized body or organization. Through funding received from the government, the MFD could (a) run accredited training schemes, including training of instructors; (b) establish accreditation linkages with suitable local and international tertiary institutions leading to a recognized qualification; and (c) ensure the development of codes of ethics and good practice. This would be a major step forward in the endeavor to professionalize the SL interpreter service in Malaysia.

REFERENCES

Bell, R. T. (1976). *Sociolinguistics: goals, approaches and problems.* London: Batsford.

Bell, R. T. (2007). Human and machine translators: A vision of 2020. *GSIT Journal of Interpreting and Translation Studies, 10* (2), 143–171.

Colin, J., & Morris, R. (1996). *Interpreters and the legal process.* Winchester, UK: Waterside Press.

Collins, J. T. (1987). Malaysian and Bazaar Malay: Polarity, continuity and communication. In Asmah Hj Omar (Ed.), *National language and communication in multilingual societies* (pp.151–174). Kuala Lumpur: Dewan Bahasa dan Pustaka.

De Jongh, E. M. (1992). *An introduction to court interpreting: Theory and practice.* Lanham, MD: University Press of America.

Domingue, R. L., & Ingram, B. L. (1978). Sign language interpretation: state of the art. In D. Gerver & H. W. Sinaiko (Eds.), *Language, interpretation and communication* (pp. 81–85). New York: Plenum.

Edwards, A. B. (1995). *The practice of court interpreting.* Amsterdam: John Benjamins.

Gammal, M. (1998). Court interpreting. In M. Baker (Ed.), *Routledge encyclopedia of translation studies* (pp. 53–56). London: Routledge.

Gonzalez, R.D., Vasquez, V. F. and Mikkelson, H. (1991) *Fundamentals of court interpretation: Theory, policy and practice.* Durham, NC: Carolina Academic Press.

Hewitt, W. E. (2002). *Court interpretation: Model guides for policy and practice in state courts.* Williamsburg, VA: National Center for State Courts.

Hymes, D. (1972). On communicative competence. In J. B. Pride, & J. Holmes (Eds.), *Sociolinguistics: Selected readings* (pp. 269–293). Harmondsworth, UK: Penguin.

Ibrahim, Z. (2002). By trial and error. *Journal of Modern Languages 14,* 113–132.

Ibrahim, Z., & Bell, R. T. (2003). Court interpreting: Malaysian perspectives. In L. Brunette, G. Bastin, I. Hemlin, & H. Clarke (Eds.), *The critical link 3* (pp. 211–222). Amsterdam: John Benjamins.

Ibrahim, Z. (2007). The interpreter as advocate: Malaysian court interpreting as a case in point. In C. Wadensjö, B. E. Dimitrova, & A-L. Nilsson (Eds.), *The critical link 4* (pp. 205–214). Amsterdam: John Benjamins.

Isham, W. P. (1998). Sign language interpreting. In M. Baker (Ed.), *Routledge encyclopedia of translation studies* (pp. 231–235). London: Routledge.

Kloss, H. (1968). Notes concerning a language-nation typology. In J. A. Fishman et al. (Eds.), *Language problems of developing nations* (pp. 69–85). New York: Wiley.

Majudiri Y Foundation for the Deaf. (2006). *Understanding deaf culture: Malaysian perspectives.* Kuala Lumpur: Author.

Mead, R. (1988). *Malaysia's language policy and legal system.* New Haven: Yale University Press.

Mikkelson, H. (2000). *Introduction to court interpreting.* Manchester: St. Jerome Publishing.

Moeketsi, R. (1999). Redefining the role of the South African court interpreter. In *Proteus 8,* (3), 2–15.

Morris, R. (1995). The moral dilemmas of court interpreters. In *The Translator 1*, (1), 35–46.

Obinna, J. (2005). *Understanding sexual violence in the Deaf Community: a preliminary report on the service provider perspective.* Retrieved June 23, 2007, from http://www.crimeandjustice.org.

Registry of Interpreters for the Deaf. (2005). *Code of professional conduct.* Retrieved August 12, 2008, from http://www.rid.org/UserFiles/File/pdfs/codeofethics.pdf.

Russell, D. (2002). *Interpreting in legal contexts: consecutive and simultaneous interpretation.* Burtonsville, MD: Linstok Press.

Teoh, S. E. (1984). *The role of interpreters in Malaysian courts.* Unpublished term paper. Faculty of Law, University of Malaya.

Wu, M. A. (1990). *The Malaysian legal system.* Petaling Jaya: Longman Malaysia.

Contributors

Zubaidah Ibrahim-Bell is an Associate Professor in the Translation Studies at the Faculty of Languages and Linguistics, University of Malaya. Her specialization is the provision of court interpreting services in Malaysia. She is currently heading a nationally funded research project on the Deaf community in Malaysia that includes the description of Malaysian Sign Language on CD and the training of interpreters. Her articles on court interpreting have been published in local journals, and internationally in the *Critical Link* series.

Bente Jacobsen is Associate Professor in the Department of Language and Business Communication at the Aarhus School of Business where she teaches court and conference interpreting to master's students of English. She is a member of the Research Group for Translating and Interpreting at the Aarhus School of Business. Her 2003 doctoral thesis (Pragmatic Meaning in Court Interpreting: An Empirical Study of Additions in Consecutively Interpreted Question-Answer Dialogues) and subsequent research has been devoted to interactional pragmatics and court interpreting. She is also a state-authorized translator and interpreter of English and works as a freelance court and conference interpreter.

Waltraud Kolb holds a research and teaching position at the Center for Translation Studies at the University of Vienna. The focus of her research is on literary translation, reception studies, and postcolonial studies. She received her PhD in comparative literature, and for many years lectured in the University of Vienna Departments of Comparative Literature and African Studies. She is a freelance translator and court-certified interpreter.

Ruth Morris is a former Brussels-based European Union staff interpreter (1972–1982). Since the early 1980s she has been a freelance interpreter and translator in Israel. While studying at the Hebrew University of Jerusalem for a master's degree in communications, she came across the English case of Iqbal Begum, a Pakistani woman whose life sentence had been successfully appealed on the ground that she had not understood the interpreter provided at a trial. This sparked an interest in interlinguistic aspects of legal proceedings, which led to her researching the impact of interpreting on legal proceedings (a project based on observations at the multilingual Demjanjuk war crimes trial) and attitudes toward court interpreters, for which she was awarded a PhD from Lancaster University, England. She is a senior lecturer at Bar-Ilan University, Israel, where she gives a research seminar in court interpreting as part of the master's program in translation and interpreting studies. She continues to nurture a faint hope that one day, just as the institution of the public defender's office in Israel arose out of a Tel Aviv University law course, the country will have a fully fledged court interpreting profession, perhaps as a result of her and her students' research. She is co-author with Joan Colin of *Interpreters and the Legal Process* (Waterside Press, 1996).

Jemina Napier is a Senior Lecturer in Translation and Interpreting in the Department of Linguistics at Macquarie University in Sydney. Jemina has almost 20 years experience of signed language interpreting in the United Kingdom and Australia. Her major research interest is in the field of signed language interpreting, but her wider interests include effective translation and interpreting pedagogy, sociolinguistics, and discourse analysis. She has published several articles discussing aspects of signed language interpreting and interpreting pedagogy. She is the author of *Sign Language Interpreting: Linguistic Coping Strategies* (Douglas McLean, 2002) and co-author, with Rachel McKee and Della Goswell, of *Sign Language Interpreting: Theory and Practice in Australia and New Zealand* (Federation Press, 2006).

Franz Pöchhacker is Associate Professor of Interpreting Studies in the Center for Translation Studies at the University of Vienna. He has worked as a freelance interpreter and conducted research on various domains of interpreting. Following his doctoral research on simultaneous conference interpreting (Simultan dolmetschen als komplexes Handeln; Gunter Narr, 1994), he has devoted most of his subsequent work to interpreting in community-based settings. He is the author of *Introducing Interpreting Studies* (Routledge, 2004) and co-editor, with Miriam Shlesinger, of *The Interpreting Studies Reader* (Routledge, 2002). They are also co-editors of *Interpreting: International Journal of Research and Practice in Interpreting.*

Debra Russell is the Director of the Western Canadian Centre for Studies in Deaf and is the David Peikoff Chair of Deafness Studies at the University of Alberta. Her primary interests include factors that affect the quality of interpretation provided between Deaf and non-deaf people, particularly in legal settings such as courtrooms, and in inclusive education settings. Dr. Russell has also been involved in research examining the needs of students with disabilities in postsecondary settings, the evaluation of interpreters in medical settings, and the creation of best practice standards for support services for Deaf and hard of hearing learners in postsecondary settings. Dr. Russell has worked with and taught interpreters across North America and has written broadly on issues of interpreter assessment, consecutive and simultaneous interpreting, and curriculum development for interpreter education programs.

Index

Aboriginal people, access of court proceedings by, 77
accuracy, x, xv, 43–44, 123, 127, 138
accuracy pledge, 9
accused's conduct, 98
acoustics, effect of, 21–22
adjudicator–interpreter team, 30
African countries, refugees from. *See* asylum appeal hearings
alternative approaches to interpretation, 6*n*3
American Sign Language (ASL), 80–81, 82. *See also* team interpreting process
archaic expressions, use of, 90
Association of Visual Language Interpreters of Canada (AVLIC), 124, 126
asylum appeal hearings, xi–xii, 26–50
  analysis, 32–46
  discussion and conclusion, 45–48
  method and data, 31–32
  research issues, 29–31
  right to seek asylum from persecution, 27–28
Attard; R. v. (1958), 23
Australia and Australian Sign Language (Auslan). *See* deaf jurors in court proceedings
Austria. *See* asylum appeal hearings
auxiliary police officers, interpreters' role as, 30
availability of interpreters, 29

backchannel feedback, 136
back translation, process of, 85, 93–99
Bahasa Isyarat Malaysia (BIM), 151. *See also* Malaysia, legal interpreting in
Bahasa Malaysia (BM), 149–50
Barsky, R., 29
Bazaar Malay, 150. *See also* Malaysia, legal interpreting in
Belgium, asylum in, 27
Berk-Seligson, S., 20, 55, 78–79, 115
borrowing, use of, 80, 93, 114
Bot, H., 41
Brennan, M., 80, 82, 93, 115
British Sign Language (BSL), 80
Brown, P., xii, 52–54, 61. *See also* face and court interpreting
Brown, R., 80, 82, 93, 115

Canada, ix, 80–81. *See also* team interpreting process
Canadian Convention refugee hearings, 29
Cartwright, B., 123
causation, explaining test for, 97
Charrow, V. R. & R. P., 83
Chechnya, refugees from, 28
Chesterman, A., 41
China, study of politeness in, 53
Chinese defendant, interpreting in non-Chinese speaking court. *See* face and court interpreting
Clark, Marsha, 2
codes of ethics, 124
co-interviewer, xi–xii, 34, 36–39, 46
Cokely, D., 123, 143
community interpreting, 29
competence, xiii, 157–61
completeness, 44–45
conferring, 133, 136
confident interpreters, 134–35
consecutive interpretation, 6, 23, 81, 127, 130
control, problem of, 2–3
cooperative principle (CP), xii–xiii, 63–64
Cotterill, J., 83

courtroom discourse
deaf jurors and. *See* deaf jurors in court proceedings
Demjanjuk trial. *See* Demjanjuk trial
face and. *See* face and court interpreting
literature review on interpretation of, 79–81
Cronin, M., 1–2
cross-cultural understanding and interpreters, 29
cultural conceptions of face, 53–54

Danet, B., 78
deaf jurors in court proceedings, xiiii–xiv, 72–122
conclusions from study, 110–13
law reform in New South Wales, Australia, 74–77
literature review, 77–84
methodology, 85–90
recommendations, 113–15
research questions, 84–85
results and discussion, 90–110
Deaf Society of New South Wales, 74
deaf witnesses, preparation conversations with, 131–35
debriefing of jurors and interpreters, 114
Demjanjuk trial, x–ix, 5–23
conclusions from, 22–23
gatekeeping and control of interpreters, 7–13
legal and linguistic details, 5–7
questions and answers, taking liberties with, 14–18
record-keeping, 13–14
speed and acoustics, 21–22
word choice, 18–20
Denmark. *See* face and court interpreting
dialogue interpreting, 30
Dies v. British & International Mining and Finance Corp. (1939), 2–3, 4–5
discourse analysis, 30, 33
discourse markers, xii–xiii, 63–64
duplicity and dynamics in court interpreting, x, 1–25
control, problem of, 2–5
Demjanjuk trial, x–ix, 5–22. *See also* Demjanjuk trial

editing, concept of, xi
Education of interpreters, 123, 124, 144, 145–46
Eichmann, Adolf, trial of, 6, 7*n*5, 11–12
endoglossic state, 149
English language
ASL interpreters and, 82
in asylum appeals. *See* asylum appeal hearings
Auslan interpreters and, 82, 84–85, 93
in Demjanjuk trial. *See* Demjanjuk trial
discourse markers in, xiii
juror competence in, 114
legal English, 78–79, 83
in Malaysia, 149, 150, 163–64
Spanish-English courtroom exchanges in U.S., 55, 79
in team interpreting process. *See* team interpreting process
error correction, use by teams of interpreters, 133, 136, 138–39, 143–44
European Convention on Human Rights, 28
expectancy norms, 41
expert witnesses, xiv, 132, 137, 141–42

face and court interpreting, xii–xiii, 51–71
analysis, 56–68
concept of face, 52–54
conclusions, 68–69
court interpreter and face, 54–56
data, 56
face in the courtroom, 54

FCICE (United States Federal Court Interpreter Certification Examination), 114
Federal Asylum Office (Austria), 28, 33
Fenton, S., 29
filler, concept of, 63
Findlay, M., 82
fingerspelling, 80, 93, 114
first person, use of, 33, 35, 41–43
forensic linguistics, 78
Frishberg, N., 123–24
frozen text, 140
functionalist translation theory, 32

Gambia, refugees from. *See* asylum appeal hearings
gatekeeping, xi, 7–13, 15, 21
Geneva Convention Relating to the Status of Refugees, 27
German, interpretation of proceedings in. *See* asylum appeal hearings; Demjanjuk trial
Germany, asylum proceedings in, 27
Gill, John, 10, 19
Goffman, E., 55
Gonzáles, R. D., 5
grammatical errors, 60
Grice, H. P., 61, 64
Guidelines for Professional Conduct, 124

Ha[illegible]1, 115
Harris, [illegible] 41
healthcare sett[illegible]rpreters in, 46, 55
Hebrew language interpreta[illegible] *See* Demjanjuk trial
Herbert, J., 5
Hernandez v. New York (1991), 3
Human Rights and Equal Opportunities Commission (New South Wales), 74
Humphrey, C., 23*n*16

Ibrahim-Bell, Z., xv–xvi, 148, 171
Illinois Pattern Instructions (IPI), 83–84
Immigration Appeals Authority (UK), 27
incompetence, effect of interpreters' fear of, xiii
Independent Federal Asylum Review Board (IFARB, Austria), 27–28. *See also* asylum appeal hearings
Inghilleri, M., 29
In re Trepca Mines Ltd. (1960), 4
institutional team, interpreter as member of, 35–36
interpreter as co-interviewer. *See* co-interviewer
interpreter preparation conversations. *See* team interpreting process
intracultural agent, interpreter as, 29
Israel, court cases in. *See* duplicity and dynamics in court interpreting
Italian Sign Language (LIS), 80
Ivan the Terrible. *See* Demjanjuk trial

Jacobsen, B., xii–xiii, 51, 171
Japan, study of politeness in, 53
Johnson, L., 124
judicial attitudes, xi, 3, 4
jurors. *See* deaf jurors in court proceedings
jury instructions, comprehension of, 83–84

Kerr, Rodney Ivan, 85–86
Kerr; Regina v. (2003), 85
Kolb, W., xi–xii, 26, 171
KTBM (manually coded *Bahasa Malaysia*), 149, 160. *See also* Malaysia, legal interpreting in

lawyer preparation for working with team interpreters, 128, 130–31, 135–40
legal discourse, literature review, 78–79

legalese, 78, 93
legal text comprehension by jurors, 83–84
Levi, J., 83–84
Levinson, S. C., xii, 52–54, 61. *See also* face and court interpreting
linguistic interpreting, 29
Lischka case, World War II war crimes trial, 18–19
literal fallacy, concept of, 160
literal translation style, 80, 93
literature review of deaf persons and court proceedings, 77–84
López, Rosa, 2, 3

Majudiri Y Foundation, 151, 154
Malaysia, legal interpreting in, ix, xv–xvi, 148–69
  languages in Malaysia, 149–51
  recommendations, 166–67
  results of questionnaire to interpreters, 156–66
  signed languages interpreting (SLI), 151–54
  study description, 154–56
Malaysian Foundation for the Deaf (MFD), 148, 154, 155–56, 167
Malaysian Signed Language (MySL), 149
Mandarin language in Malaysia, 149, 163
manslaughter, 96–97
Mather, S. & R., 82
Maurer-Kober, B., 30–31, 35
McCay, V., 77–78
McKee, D., 73–74
meaning, concept of, 131
medical interviews, concept of face in, 55
"mere cypher," interpreters as, 23
Mikkelson, H., 5
Miller, K., 77–78
mock trials, use of, 80–81, 115. *See also* team interpreting process
Morris, R., x–ix, 1, 6*n*3, 171–72
mouthing, use of, 80, 93, 114
multiple language speakers, interpretation of trial for. *See* Demjanjuk trial

naïve language user fallacy, 160
Napier, J., xiiii–xiv, 72, 172
National Accreditation Authority for Translators and Interpreters (NAATI) qualifications, 114
"necessary evil," concept of, 5
negative politeness, concept of, 53
nervousness, 133–34
neutral and invisible, interpreter's role as, 30, 35–36, 47
neutral linguistic mediators, 45
New South Wales (NSW), Australia. *See* deaf jurors in court proceedings
New South Wales Association of the Deaf, 74
New Zealand
  deaf jurors in, 73–74, 81
  refugees in, 29
  Sign Language (NZSL) Bill, 73–74
Nigeria, refugees from. *See* asylum appeal hearings
non-deaf lawyers, preparation conversations with, 128, 130–31, 135–40
non-person, impression of courtroom interpreter as, 55
Nord, C., 32
North America, hiring and education practices in, 123, 124. *See also specific countries*
notetaking by interpreters, 127, 134, 141
NSW Association of the Deaf, 74
NSW Law Reform Commission (NSWLRC), 74–76, 115

oaths, 140
O'Connor, Mark, 7–9, 14, 17–18, 21–22
"official translation" of trial testimony, 3

parties, references to, 90, 93
People With Disabilities (New South Wales), 74
Permanent Commission of Appeal for Refugees (Belgium), 27
Pöchhacker, F., xi–xii, 26, 129, 172
police officer cautions, comprehensibility of, 83
politeness, theory of, xii, 52–53
Pöllabauer, S., 30, 31, 34, 35, 36, 40, 47
positive face, concept of. *See* face and court interpreting
predictive screen test, 114
preparation process and team interpreters. *See* team interpreting process
professionalism issues in team interpreting, 144
professional norms, 41–45, 47, 165–66
pronouns, unclear use of, 93
public self-image, 52. *See also* face and court interpreting

quality, maxim of, 61, 64
quality hedge, 61
Quirk, R., 61

Rajnowski v. Detroit (1889), 4, 14
reasonable and proportionate, defining, 98, 99
record of proceedings, 13–14, 34, 39–41, 47, 152
Refugee Status Appeals Authority (New Zealand), 29
refugee status determination. *See* asylum appeal hearings
Registry for Interpreters of the Deaf (RID), 124, 163
response markers, 64
roles and participation status in proceedings, xvi, 30, 34–41, 46, 82, 164–65
Russell, D., xiv–xv, 80–81, 115, 123, 139, 172–73
Russian language, use in asylum proceedings in Austria, 28

Sabah Association of Women (SAWO), 162, 163
Scheffer, T., 30, 36, 47
Schein, J., 123
Schiffrin, D., 63, 64
Schnier v. People (1859), 3, 4
Shaffer, B., 131
Shaw, R., 123–24
Shlesinger, M., 9
signals, use by teams of interpreters, 127–28, 136
Simpson, O. J., murder trial of, 2, 3
simultaneous interpretation, 23, 81, 130
Skopos theory, 32, 46
Spanish-English court room exchanges in U.S., 55, 79
speed and acoustics, effect of, 21–22
Spencer, D., xiiii–xiv, 72
Spencer-Oatey, H., 53–54
spokesperson, designation of, 130
Stewart, D., 123
support by interpreter team members, 127, 136, 139

tag questions, xii, 61–62
Tamil language in Malaysia, 149
team interpreting process, xiv–xv, 123–47
  conclusion of study, 81, 144–46
  data analysis and findings, 127–35
  discussion, 142–44
  implications for teams of interpreters, 140–42
  interpreter educators and interpreters, implications for, 144
  judge and lawyer interview results, 135–40
  results, 135–40
  study objectives, method, and participants, 125–26
tests for court interpreters, 114

third grammatical person, use of, xii, 15
translational norms, xii, 14–22. *See also* accuracy
fidelity, 47–48
translation vs. interpretation, defined, 2*n*1
treason and interpreting. *See* duplicity and dynamics in court interpreting
Treblinka death camp guard, trial of. *See* Demjanjuk trial
Trepca Mines Ltd., In re (1960), 4
true interpreter norm, 41
trust issues in team interpreting, 125, 144. *See also* team interpreting process

Ukrainian language, interpretation of. *See* Demjanjuk trial
unconscious motivation, 20
United Kingdom
asylum application system in, 29
deaf jurors in, 73
deaf people's access to justice in, 80
police interviewing practices in, xi
refugee status determination, 27
United Nations High Commissioner for Refugees (UNHCR), 27
United Nations (UN), 27
United States
court interpreting in, 3, 5
deaf jurors in, 73, 81
English-Spanish court room exchanges in, 55, 79
federal court interpreter certification in, 114
juror comprehension, future research and, 115
non-English speaking jurors in, 81
RID in, 163
United States Court Interpreters Act (1978), 114
United States Federal Court Interpreter Certification Examination (FCICE), 114
Universal Declaration of Human Rights, 27

Vásquez, V., 5
verbally allying with adjudicator, 34
verbatim standard of performance for interpreters, 5, 13–14
views of interpreting models, 129–30

Wadensjö, Cecilia, 30, 33, 55
"well," use as marker, xii–xiii, 63–64
whispering interpretation, 23
Wilcox, S., 131
witness preparation. *See also* expert witnesses
of deaf witnesses, 131–35
Witter-Merithew, A., 124
Wood, James, 83
word choice in interpreting, 18–20
work sharing in teams of interpreters, 127
World War II death camp guard. *See* Demjanjuk trial
written directions, clarifying, 98–99

Yiddish language, interpretation of. *See* Demjanjuk trial
YMCA Kuala Lumpur, 151

Zeisel, H., 84
Zimbabwe, refugees from. *See* asylum appeal hearings